Raymond Barfield

The Poetic Apriori:
Philosophical Imagination in a Meaningful Universe

STUDIES IN HISTORICAL PHILOSOPHY

Editor: Alexander Gungov

Consulting Editor: Donald Phillip Verene

ISSN 2629-0316

1 *Dustin Peone*
   Memory as Philosophy
   The Theory and Practice of Philosophical Recollection
   ISBN 978-3-8382-1336-1

2 *Raymond Barfield*
   The Poetic Apriori: Philosophical Imagination in a Meaningful Universe
   ISBN 978-3-8382-1350-7

Raymond Barfield

THE POETIC APRIORI: PHILOSOPHICAL IMAGINATION IN A MEANINGFUL UNIVERSE

Bibliografische Information der Deutschen Nationalbibliothek
Die Deutsche Nationalbibliothek verzeichnet diese Publikation in der Deutschen Nationalbibliografie; detaillierte bibliografische Daten sind im Internet über http://dnb.d-nb.de abrufbar.

Bibliographic information published by the Deutsche Nationalbibliothek
Die Deutsche Nationalbibliothek lists this publication in the Deutsche Nationalbibliografie; detailed bibliographic data are available in the Internet at http://dnb.d-nb.de.

ISBN-13: 978-3-8382-1350-7
© *ibidem*-Verlag, Stuttgart 2019
Alle Rechte vorbehalten

Das Werk einschließlich aller seiner Teile ist urheberrechtlich geschützt. Jede Verwertung außerhalb der engen Grenzen des Urheberrechtsgesetzes ist ohne Zustimmung des Verlages unzulässig und strafbar. Dies gilt insbesondere für Vervielfältigungen, Übersetzungen, Mikroverfilmungen und elektronische Speicherformen sowie die Einspeicherung und Verarbeitung in elektronischen Systemen.

All rights reserved. No part of this publication may be reproduced, stored in or introduced into a retrieval system, or transmitted, in any form, or by any means (electronic, mechanical, photocopying, recording or otherwise) without the prior written permission of the publisher. Any person who does any unauthorized act in relation to this publication may be liable to criminal prosecution and civil claims for damages.

Printed in the EU

For Julia

For Julia

Table of Contents

Preface 9

I. Imagination and Our Experience of the Universe 15

II. Imagination and Our Knowledge of Creation and God 29

III. Imagination and the Holy 43

IV. Imagination and Love.. 55

V. Imagination and Mythic Discovery.................................... 67

VI. Imagination and Created Things...................................... 85

VII. Imagination and the Lonely Mind.................................... 99

VIII. Imagination and Partnership with God to Create a World 113

IX. Imagination and Seeing through Naming 133

X. Imagination and the Analogia Entis................................. 149

Biblography 165

Index 167

Preface

Exploring the nature of imagination and its role in our search for meaning is a philosophical act. To understand the imagination, we must look at what it makes. In science, philosophy, literature, and art, the imagination leaves artifacts in its wake. These artifacts express the truth, significance, and meaning we discover in the universe. But knowing these expressive artifacts is not enough if we want to understand the imagination. We also need to understand the *significance* of significance, the *meaning* of meaning, and the ways in which matter can *matter*, all of which depend on how we answer questions about what kind of universe we live in.

In this book I argue that many of our most valuable inquiries are acts of philosophical imagination, that the artifacts of the imagination make most sense in a universe that is meaningful as a whole, and that only a created universe has meaning as a whole. My arguments do not prove that the universe *is* meaningful as a whole. They only explore ways the imagination might be characterized *were* the universe to be meaningful as a whole. Apart from the assumption that the universe is created, some theories of the imagination make no sense whatsoever. But if the universe is created, these theories might illuminate the status and function of the imagination, along with the relationship between imagination and our experience of beauty, morality, metaphysics, and science.

I organize my argument around the concept of the *poetic apriori*, which is the idea that artifacts of the imagination can reveal as-yet unknown aspects of reality. It is the idea that the imagination can reveal *reality* through what it *makes*. The idea started out a bit tongue-in-cheek while I was writing a novel about Immanuel Kant's servant, Martin Lampe. Lampe lived with a philosophical genius for forty years, until he was fired for reasons no one knows. He surely listened in on philosophical conversations and lectures, and no doubt he had the chance to snoop around Kant's books-in-progress with relative freedom. Because that probably constitutes the longest tutelage in the history of Western philosophy, I needed to give Lampe at least one idea he could claim as his own: in the novel I gifted him with the idea of the poetic apriori. But the more I thought about the idea, the more I liked it. Lampe can still have it in the world of fiction, but I decided to see where the idea might go in the slightly less fictional world I call "my life." To that end I have borrowed from scientists, artists, poets, and philosophers to illustrate how the idea of the poetic apriori might function in a theory of philosophical imagination. The first nine chapters gesture toward the relationships between imagination, intellect, and meaning that emerge through the operation of the poetic apriori. The discussion builds toward a final argument that the operation of the poetic apriori in the work of philosophical imagination is possible because of a deep structure in reality that is most fully revealed in the idea of the *analogia entis.*

Chapter one begins with an example of an Aristotelian frame for the relationship of the mind to the material and the immaterial aspects of the world. We are embodied creatures susceptible to many physically determined forces, and yet our minds can abstract forms from the physical shapes of things, and we can grasp immaterial meanings through the physical shapes of words and numbers. The ways our minds relate to material and immaterial parts of the world is important for understanding our peculiar form of philosophical imagination. It is also important for understanding the difference between the realms of meaning, freedom, and rationality, and the world of fully determined material causation investigated by the sciences. A robust view of the world as created makes sense of the idea that the forms of nature are readable by human beings, not because the forms are imposed by our minds but because the outward material world is informed by the immaterial—by thought of the same sort that populates our own minds. If our imaginations are created by God, our minds can reach into the darkness of the unknown, trusting not merely in the light we carry within us but also in the wisdom, truth, and beauty of an in-formed creation.

The second chapter turns to the concept of analogy. Analogy, as an idea fostered among the ancient Greeks, matured into the idea of the analogia entis in Thomas Aquinas's philosophical investigation. Thomas came to see that if creation is an effect of God, then a metaphysics of creation cannot say creation is wholly alien to God. But neither can it say creation is wholly like the creator. Because creation is both similar and dissimilar to God, creation must be a kind of analogy, the analogy of being. This idea acknowledges the similarity between God and creation, as well as the dissimilarity between them. Though the method of the analogia entis, we attempt to comprehend the whole from within the whole that comprehends us. Analogical philosophy discovers reality through lenses made in the philosophical imagination. It is revised as our consciousness of all that lies beyond our current knowledge and experience grows. Things light up in the fullness of being what they are, and in doing so they also point beyond themselves. This is *analogical* distance. It allows us to know creation *as* creation. Analogy always falls short, which is why the trajectory of philosophical work often arcs toward silent wonder. But even if the work leads us to silence before incomprehensible mystery, we are creatures who desire to know and to share what we discover, which are acts of philosophical imagination.

If the universe is created, philosophical imagination and the significance of its artifacts might be influenced by the way in which our imaginations relate to God. The first half of chapter three draws on several themes from the work of Thomas Raymond Kelly to illustrate this. At the center of Kelly's philosophical work is the idea that our encounters with God shape our imaginations. One's spiritual life impacts the growth of an imagination that aims to discover what is real. The second half of the chapter turns to Charles Peguy whose imaginative artifacts are a result of an imagination oriented in the way that Kelly suggests.

Expanding on the ideas in chapter three, chapter four examines the ways in which acts of love might impact the function of the imagination and the things it makes. Dante inhabited his imagination as a lover. He filled his poetry with images exemplifying a mind oriented toward divine significance in the universe. But because any image can become an idol, as Dante knew well, the argument turns to Bonaventure to explore how love can motivate and enable a kind of imaginative growth that resists both idolatry and philosophical stasis.

Chapter five looks at a very different way of framing philosophical imagination in a created universe developed in the work of Giambattista Vico. For Vico, there is a deep division between ways the imagination understands God and creation, and the ways the imagination understands things that are of human origin such as history and language. This part of the argument begins with Vico's theory of the imagination and its relationship to memory and then develops the theme of memory and its relationship to imagination in the works of Giordano Bruno and Giullo Camillo.

If imagination is capable of genuine discovery in a created world, what is it actually seeing in the world? To begin an answer to this question, chapter six turns to Gerard Manley Hopkins and the ideas of instress and inscape in his poetry and prose. For Hopkins, there was no clear line between natural and supernatural perception of the creator and creation, and both his poetry and his poetics use the analogia entis as a frame for understanding the reality of things that appear in creation.

Chapter seven approaches questions similar to those in chapter six but from the perspective of Wallace Stevens—a poet who thought deeply about the role of imagination in our conscious navigation of the world and our own minds, but who viewed the possibility of God as "the supreme fiction." For Stevens, the world is made from the senses and imagination. This is the origin of the poet's power. But a peculiar view of the power of the imagination for both poet and philosopher emerges in Stevens's poetry and prose. Though he is not a theist, the idea of God plays a crucial role in his theory of the imagination. Because of this, his theory resonates surprisingly with that of Hopkins.

Chapter eight turns to the construction of a view of imagination that draws on the previous two chapters. The poet seeks to forge a bridge between what is real and what is made in the cauldron of lived experience. Stevens was pessimistic about anything that might be construed as an ontologically substantial frame for human purposes or ends. But if his theory of the imagination is imported into a theistic view of the universe, the theory functions in a way that is similar to the function of the analogia entis prominently featured in Hopkins's theory. From the model formed through the work of these two poets, the argument moves to the model developed by Alfred North Whitehead, for whom the imagination's role in any exploration of reality requires that we think about propositions as a hybrid between potentiality and actuality. For Whitehead, only the properly formed imagination allows us to see patterns in the humanities and sciences where we might otherwise remain blind.

Chapter nine takes the insight with which chapter eight concludes, and turns to T. S. Eliot and Owen Barfield. These two thinkers expand upon the imagination's role in helping us to see meaning in patterns. They show how language is both the storehouse of the imagination and one instrument with which the imagination grows its insights into reality. The veracity of the imagination's discoveries through language depends upon the kind of universe we live in. If the universe is created we have reason to trust in the truth-finding activity of the imagination. If the universe erupts without purpose or end from nothing, we will have a very different assessment of the value of the imagination's "discoveries."

Chapter ten brings together the picture of the imagination developed in the first nine chapters, and it gathers them under the idea of the analogia entis. By analogy we understand the relationship between creator and creature. We may begin with sense experience, but in a created universe, the idea of a holy order that orients the universe as a whole transforms the frame in which we understand sense experience and the way in which we move from the concreteness of the immanent to the idea of the transcendent. Through the function of the poetic apriori, the artifacts of philosophical imagination reach toward what lies beyond our experience of the world and express the ordered connections—the underlying Word, the Logos—discovered through these imaginative acts. The analogia entis is the principle that lends optimism to that work, and the principle only makes sense in a created universe that is meaningful as a whole.

I am deeply grateful to Donald Verene, Alexander Gungov, and Julia Klein for their comments on various versions of the manuscript, and to Erin Elizabeth Williams for her extraordinary help in editing the book and bringing it to completion. I have learned that no matter how many times a manuscript is read, mistakes, lapses, and blind spots still find their way in, and I am responsible for any that persist despite best efforts.

I. Imagination and Our Experience of the Universe

Leibniz asked a good question. Why does something exist rather than nothing?[1]

Granting that things exist, Leibniz thinks we should be able to give a reason why they exist—his concept of the principle of sufficient reason, which he develops in *Monadology* and in *Theodicy*. His question has occupied many philosophers after him. Hegel, who was a master of philosophical imagination, began his *Science of Logic* with a discussion of the concepts of *being*, *nothing*, and the way something passes from nothingness into being through *becoming*.[2] Martin Heidegger called it the fundamental question of metaphysics.[3] Though Ludwig Wittgenstein thought verbal expressions of awe are often nonsense, he also thought the feeling of awe is of absolute significance to human beings. He wrote, "6.44 Not *how* the world is, is the mystical, but *that* it is."[4]

Irrespective of the way one interprets the terms of the question, overfamiliarity can lead a thinker to miss the substantial imaginative act required to fully grasp Leibniz's question.

First, try to imagine nothing.

No objects. No minds. No time.

No forces, no vacuum, no space, no laws.

Nothing.

It requires focus and patience. Once you have succeeded in imagining nothing, try to imagine one thing—a single atom, say—popping into

---

[1] I am grateful to Donald Verene for directing me to the first place where Leibniz makes this statement in his essay, "Principes de la nature et de la grâce, fondés en raison," written in 1714, the same year as his *Monadologie*. The essay is available in Gottfried Wilhelm Leibniz, *The Monadology and Other Philosophical Writings*, trans. Robert Latta, Kessinger Publishing, Montana (2010), 405-24.

[2] Georg Wilhelm Friedrich Hegel, *The Science of Logic*, trans. George Di Giovanni, Cambridge University Press, Cambridge (2015).

[3] Martin Heidegger, *An Introduction to Metaphysics*, trans. Gregory Fried and Richard Polt, Yale University Press, New Haven and London (2014), 1-4.

[4] Ludwig Wittgenstein, *Tractatus Logico-Philosophicus*, trans. Charles Kay Ogden, Routledge Press, New York (1981), 187.

existence from nothing. Then, think about the difference between nothing and the single thing that now exists. This is one way a universe might occur. It might have had a beginning, coming into existence from nothing. The alternative is that something has existed without beginning, eternally—perhaps the universe itself, the stuff from which the universe came, or a divinity who created the universe. In any case, there might have been nothing, from which something came, or else the universe (or its source) might have always existed. Both answers are as strange as Leibniz's question. We cannot escape strangeness.

Every argument has a starting point, often involving a choice between two possibilities that take the logical form of P or $\sim P$. Either the universe had a beginning or it did not. Either it has an end or it does not. Either it is created or it is not created. Even if the motivation for choosing a starting point is unclear, an argument can still be illuminating in a "What if this were true?" kind of way. As we compare the argument's consequences to our lived experience, we can ask whether experience makes the starting points seem more compelling, or less.

Victor Hugo described the universe as an appearance corrected by a transparency. *Correction* is the story we tell about the universe. It affects the way we see things in the universe, and it may even affect whether or not we are aware of a thing in the first place. Theories of philosophical imagination are about the meaning of the word correction. The nature of philosophical imagination is disclosed through iterative imaginative acts that form a story about what shows up in our experience. Each imaginative act is a variation on the question, "What if this were true?" Certain ways of conceiving imagination that are plausible in one kind of universe are implausible (or even nonsense) in another kind.

For example, assume the universe is uncreated but had a beginning: once there was nothing, and then, as a brute *just so* fact, there was something. Over time this something moved from its initial state to its current state, part of which is the existence of people like us who have minds. At some point, we began telling stories about the origin and meaning of the universe. Divine characters appeared in many of the stories—characters that were sometimes identified with celestial bodies such as stars, sometimes identified with forces that arise in the natural world, and sometimes distilled into complex visions of God such as those found in Islam, Judaism, and Christianity. But if God does not exist, we need a correction to bring our story of the universe into better accord with our assumptions about what is real.

Deciding which assumptions should guide revisions to our stories is sometimes viewed as the task of modern science. This is a category mistake: embracing an assumption that limits the possible stories we can tell about the universe is a philosophical act rather than a scientific act. But the mistake is understandable. When we use scientific methods to study appearances in the sky, for example, we discover that the stars and the forces affecting the stars are mathematically describable physical phenomena. Scientific models based on our observations allow us to predict the behavior of these phenomena reliably without introducing personal forces in the form of God or other divine creative entities. If science can cleanse mythological personal forces from our astronomy, perhaps the same correction will hold for the rest of the universe.

What if we apply our corrective transparency to other personal forces in the universe? Does this kind of correction eliminate all people from the universe? At first, the answer to this question seems to be *No*, simply because there are apparently persons in the universe who have force—ourselves, for example. But there are also reasons for answering *Yes*. Prior to the appearance of people, non-personal reality constituted all that exists. If reality prior to the appearance of people was non-personal, the personal arose from the non-personal. When people appeared in the universe, they were simply a new arrangement of non-personal stuff that resulted in the kinds of things we associate with persons—activities such as love, longing, science, philosophy, and storytelling. But because all of these things arose from the non-personal, the activities of people are at the deepest level nothing more than another way to arrange non-personal, accidental, purposeless stuff. What else could they be?

Such an account requires enormous imaginative activity. A theory is a kind of story about something. Every attempt to build a coherent theory about reality is an act of imagination. Because there is actually stuff in the universe behaving in certain ways, we can test our scientific theories about the universe and assess their predictive value. If a theory we have imagined provides a satisfying explanation for the ways past and present events appear to us, and if it accurately predicts how future events will show up, we are justified in thinking our theory is pretty good. If some part of our theory can be eliminated without changing the robustness of our account of everything past, present, and future, then that part of the theory is doing no work. In the spirit of Ockham's razor, perhaps it should be lopped off.

I say *perhaps* it should be lopped off, because the choice to lop it off is a philosophical, or even aesthetic, choice: we like theories in which all the parts do some kind of work, and we often prefer simplicity to complexity, all other things being equal. But the universe might actually be full of useless parts that do no work at all. If so, lopping off parts will make our theory neater, but it will not get us closer to the truth of the universe.

If something shows up that cannot be accounted for by our theory, then our theory is incomplete. We must imagine a better one, or at least remain open to the possibility that another theory might be better. Imagination depends upon our openness to possibility. Although a theist can consistently commit to any theory about the origin of the universe, including theories in which the universe exists independently of divine action, the assumption that there is no God limits the possibilities to which we can reasonably remain open. Nonetheless, there are good reasons to assume there is no God. We once thought gods dwelt on the mountaintop, but when we climbed the mountain, we found no gods. We once thought celestial bodies were divinities, but when we created telescopes and rockets to explore the universe, we found no gods. And so, when we turn to other things that show up, including people and the activities and experiences associated with people, we might reasonably assume that a complete story can be told without invoking the existence of God. It is an assumption, simply because the story is still incomplete. But we must make some assumptions because our time is limited, and so our storytelling must likewise be limited. Clarifying these limits is the work of philosophy. Defining limits for imaginative reach is a philosophical task.

In my discussion of philosophical imagination, I will begin with a different assumption. I will assume the universe is created, and I will consider how the assumption that the universe is created affects theories of philosophical imagination. The assumption illuminates some ideas that would make no sense without it. It marks the difference between a universe that has no inherent meaning or purpose (however meaningful it might *seem* to creatures like us) and a universe that might have inherent meaning and purpose as a whole (because it was created).

We will never reach a bedrock of Cartesian certainty about our assumptions, because we never reach a bedrock of Cartesian certainty about anything. But we can still test theories against human experience, as long as we avoid asking of experience something it is incapable of delivering. Instruments for testing the sugar content of grapes aid in the craft of winemaking. But we are sure to be disappointed if try to use our sugar-testing instruments to measure the overall quality of the wine. For that we must taste the wine, maybe with guidance from an experienced sommelier.

The same is true for philosophical investigation. Suppose, for example, that the imagination functions to bring the cosmos into the soul, allowing the significance of things to take hold. For this theory to be true, of course, things that appear—stars, persons, the universe as a whole—must actually have significance. The presence or absence of such significance cannot be tested through scientific experimentation. A soul is required to register significance. Such a theory of the imagination, however strange, leads to surprising possibilities. Perhaps significance in the cosmos can only be perceived by a prayer-formed imagination. Perhaps the universe has been waiting for our form of imaginative seeing, just as God waited for Adam to name the animals (Genesis 2:19): "Out of the ground the Lord God formed every animal of the field and every bird of the air, and brought them to the man to see what he would call them; and whatever the man called every living creature, that was its name." Naming is an imaginative act of the soul that has real power in the world. It changes our ability to see the significance and meaning of things. Naming both reveals and contributes to reality.

Even if we assume the universe is created, ideas of this sort are speculative. They can be tested against human experience to confirm or disconfirm our sense of their veracity. But just as we rely on a sommelier to assess the quality of wine, to test a theory of the imagination in which the soul, the cosmos, and human purpose converge with our pursuit of knowledge about God, we may need guidance from a theological poet or a saint, rather than a scientist. Because God is unfathomable by finite creatures such as ourselves, the work of imaginative reach is never finished, and neither is all that follows from imaginative acts—artistic, literary, and liturgical expressions of imaginative discoveries, along with scientific, philosophical, and theological theories.

Imaginative acts leave artifacts in their wake. Theories, poems, paintings, music, relationships—these artifacts are traces that hint at the nature of the imagination and its relationship to the world. The artifacts are made (*poesis*), but they can reveal reality. They are in the same category as Adam's naming of the animals. Insofar as things exist before they are named, existence is prior to the imaginative act. But insofar as naming allows a thing to be seen or to be seen in a certain way, the imaginative act of naming is prior to our experience of a thing as it shows up in the world. Naming has priority in theories of the imagination that allow the soul to receive appearances and to register significance coinciding with a thing's proper name. The place of the *made* in the discovery of the *true* is what I mean by the term at the heart of this theory of philosophical imagination—the *poetic apriori*. The coherence of the idea of the poetic apriori, in turn, depends upon the organizing idea around which the entire theory is developed—the *analogia entis*, the analogy of being.

The idea of the soul is a placeholder for whatever it is that allows us to perceive, to investigate, and to discover the significance of things through the imagination in a created universe. The soul's response to everything imagination imports or creates illuminates the power and purpose of the imagination. The forms, patterns, and contours of what the imagination makes are determined by the reality the imagination encounters, along with the character, limits, power, and function of the imagination itself. The soul registers the truth of what the imagination makes. Without the artifacts of the imagination, the soul would be isolated from reality. But without the soul, truth cannot emerge from imaginative acts, just as truth does not emerge in the words produced by a computer algorithm unless there is a reader to register the presence or absence of meaning. The idea of the poetic apriori gestures toward the conditions required for the imagination to have the power to make artifacts that enable the soul to see reality. The soul craves truth that aligns with reality. It loves wisdom, and it desires to know both itself and the world around it.

Some theories of the imagination make more sense in an uncreated universe than in a created universe. In such theories, the imagination is a byproduct of accidental, purposeless events, because ultimately everything is a byproduct of accidental, purposeless events. These theories are not my concern. My entire discussion of the philosophical imagination depends upon the assumption that the universe is created, because the theory depends upon a kind of significance that things can have only in a universe that is meaningful as a whole.

We show up in the world. As we develop self-awareness, most of us have a sense of ourselves as a whole, rather than merely a collection of parts. Many of us also have a sense of being a single person over time. We feel at least the temporary unity of our being, even if its foundation is not apparent to us. In between this mysterious ground and everything we encounter in the cosmos, we have an inner world where experiences meet in sense, memory, and imagination. Everything that populates this vast inner world is open to our exploration through thought, feeling, and perhaps other forms of intimate awareness. This is the theater of our soul.

In this arena, between the visible and the invisible, we explore, shape, and revise our experience of the world. All the facts of the world show up here. The meaning of the world also shows up here. As we discover the texture of the world, we become aware of something beyond the experience of discrete data points. Imagination allows us to reach outward, inward, and upward for what is not yet known—sometimes wonderful, sometimes frightening, sometimes uncanny. It is a power both to project and to receive. When it projects, the result is sometimes mere fiction. But even fiction can transform our ability to see, for better or worse.

As we come up against the fullness of reality in the theater of our souls, we correct our partial vision with the transparencies we make and lay on the world. Our transparencies are likewise revised by our perception of significance in the world, which changes the way we see things. There is no end to revision in the sense of completeness, but there is an end to revision and imaginative reach in the sense of a purpose, a direction, a *telos*. Imaginative revision often takes the form of play. This is not a denigration of imaginative work but rather an exaltation of play as a means of discovery. Imaginative play is a response to the peculiar beckoning that we experience as significance or beauty, the meaning of the whole.

The philosophical imagination is a faculty for discovering significance through a certain kind of making. Rationality is, in part, our ability to question and to test these discoveries. Rationality—like the ideas of imagination and soul—is a placeholder for something with real force in a person's inward life and in a person's interaction with reality. Our accounts of reality, constructed through our imaginative acts of naming and making, can only approximate truth as far as we know. The boundaries of real things often seem hazy to us. But the work of philosophical imagination is still useful. And besides, we cannot avoid it. We are compelled to name the things in our world, to name their forms as they appear to us. This is one of our most important sources of knowledge.

If naming is an imaginative act that gives us genuine insight into reality and if rationality is, at least in part, how we test imagination's artifacts, what is the relationship of the soul to imagination and rationality? Answering this question requires a larger philosophical context to avoid reducing the imagination to something that is not imagination. If the imagination brings candidates for significance to the soul, the idea of the soul itself is surely one of those candidates. There are many concepts of the soul consistent with the theory of imagination I am developing. I will briefly consider an Aristotelian account of the soul because it is accessible and requires fewer religious commitments than some other accounts.[5] This discussion is meant primarily to demonstrate one compelling approach to discussing the soul, but other accounts would serve my central arguments about philosophical imagination just as well.

The imagination suggests things to us. Think of it as an instrument that is sensitive to reverberations unfelt by other aspects of the mind. It listens for the echoes of our own calls, bounced back to us by the surfaces of real things, as we grope our way along in the shadow lands, moving farther in and farther up. Imagination uses hope, play, metaphor, and analogy to explore. Through these imaginative acts, we discover the vast treasure trove that is the soul. The contour of the soul appears through its unification of the value, significance, and there-ness of our active presence in the world. It turns the universe into a university. Along the way, one early discovery is that we do not have a soul. We are a soul.

Aristotle described humans as rational animals who use concepts as tools to reason about things we cannot observe. Material bodies and brains are a necessary, but not sufficient, condition for our ability to use concepts. Immaterial intellect is also needed. Without intellect, we cannot use concepts.

To understand the non-material nature of our intellect, we must understand the difference between form and shape. A form is the essential nature of the thing. It is the answer to the question, *What is it?* A shape is a complete, quantifiable description of the thing. The sciences study shapes because shape is the totality of a thing's quantifiable properties, and science studies quantifiable properties.

The soul is the form of the body, not its shape. When neuroscientists dissect the brain but find no soul and then conclude that either the soul is nothing other than the material of the brain, or that souls do not exist, they have confused form and shape. The Aristotelian point is that souls exist, but they are not the same as material substances, nor do they exist in the gaps between material substances.

Aristotle distinguished three kinds of souls based on their essential abilities: there are souls that make bodies alive, souls that make animals both alive and sentient (which means they can feel, though there is no

---

[5] I will borrow from the clear, if controversial, Aristotelian arguments Ric Machuga makes in his book, *In Defense of the Soul: What it Means to Be Human* [Brazos Press, Michigan (2002)]. His book is a thoughtful and well-written example of an effort to engage contemporary philosophy and culture from within an Aristotelian frame.

threshold between souls with faint feelings and souls that respond intensely to *The Goldberg Variations*), and souls capable of life, consciousness, and self-knowledge. These latter souls, of which we are examples, can use language to abstract forms from shapes. This allows us to reason about things unseen and unexperienced (such as God, whom we have never seen, and death, which we have never experienced).

Shapes can be pictured, but forms can only be conceived. Forms divide matter ontologically. These formal divisions are inaccessible to science *qua* science, though not to a scientist *qua* human. The difference between a shape and a form is a difference of kind, not degree. Forms can never be reduced to shapes. Ontological differences in kind coexist with biological continuity. There are naturally occurring ontological distinctions between elements, compounds, plants, animals, and humans (or human-like creatures). The lower kinds touch the higher, so there is some fuzziness in classification. It might be hard to say at what point organic compounds can first register feeling, but this epistemological fuzziness is compatible with ontological sharpness. At whatever stage the feeling shows up, once it does, there is a new kind of thing. A thing that is capable of feeling is a different kind of thing than a thing that is not capable of feeling, even though the phylogenetic continuum is not interrupted.

Of the four types of causes Aristotle identified—material, formal, efficient, and final—philosophy is primarily interested in formal and final causality. It offers a clarifying question that fits well with an understanding of the imagination and the soul that asks, "Can we understand the significance of the universe in which we live?" The search for magical elements in the gaps between efficient causes will never lead to a grasp of the beauty of music, the meaning of words, or the information stored on a computer, because these things have to do with the form of a thing, not its shape. To see beauty, meaning, or information we must look beyond mechanism. The difference between seeing an efficient cause and seeing a final cause is the difference between perceiving and conceiving, the difference between empirical induction and conceptual induction.

Empirical induction is the form of reasoning that moves from observed events to connections between these events. Chemical A is mixed with chemical B and reaction X occurs. We conclude that the chemical mixing of A and B caused the reaction X. This is the work of science. It is also the target for David Hume's famous skepticism. Hume argued that experience can tell us nothing beyond the constant conjunction of events. Event one: chemical A is mixed with chemical B. Event two: reaction X occurs. This says nothing about a causal relation between the two events. To conclude that event X is caused by mixing chemical A and chemical B, we must assume the first principle of empirical inductive reasoning, which is that everything has a cause—*nothing* comes from nothing. But this assumption depends upon rational insight, which is not itself a result of empirical induction.

Empirical induction concerns causal events. Conceptual induction concerns the purposes and forms of things. Rational insight allows conceptual induction, allows us to see forms as forms, and even allows us to understand things that have no extension. Without rational insight into form, we would be no better than video recorders, with no insight into the thingness of recorded things. We would not understand the functions, interactions, and purposes of things. Recording and seeing are very different.

Questions of purpose or form cannot be answered without reference to final causes. This is important for any kind of thinking, including the kind of thinking we call science. Aristotle had a robust notion of biology. He thought that biologists should strive to include both efficient and final causes in their description of the world. In his discussion of the soul, Machuga uses the example of a turtle to illustrate this point. We can say, "The turtle came ashore *to* lay her eggs," and we can say, "The turtle came ashore *and* laid her eggs." The first statement illuminates nature in a way the second statement does not, because the second statement cannot be distinguished from, "The turtle came ashore *and* kicked the sand," or "The turtle came ashore *and* reflected a photon into the eyes of an owl."

Similar points can be made in the realm of molecular biology, regarding the presence of information in the genetic code. Machuga illustrates the significance of information with a simple example. Suppose we are invited to a party on the beach. We are instructed to park and then to walk in the direction of the arrow the organizers will place on the beach, using driftwood to make the arrow. We park, walk to the beach, and there on the sand is an arrow made of driftwood, pointing to our right. We walk to the right, join the party, and have a wonderful time. Now, suppose that our friends arrange the arrow, but the waves come up and swallow the sticks. Then a second large wave accidentally deposits two sticks arranged in an arrow pointing to the right. We park, walk to the beach, and there on the sand is an arrow made of driftwood, pointing to our right. We walk to the right, join the party, and have a wonderful time.

The two scenarios illustrate the relationship between efficient causes (operative in both scenarios) and final causes (operative only in the first scenario). The relationship between efficient and final causes is important for understanding the implications of molecular biology. Is DNA a real embedded genetic code? Is it information? Aristotelians hold that physical objects can only function as if they are a code when they are situated in a world where other things with the same or similar physical shapes really are a code.

This raises an important question. Can something that began as nothing more than, say, a physical flaw in a crystal, containing no more information than any other crack in a rock, become information over time? Aristotle would say no for the following reason: If DNA is a code, it is functioning as a kind of language that preserves and transmits information. The words in any language are physical things, but they are not just physical things—they have a form. The forms of words are concepts we intentionally impose on physical patterns. Concepts are immaterial, and they exist only in the immaterial minds of people. Concepts are not *in* words the way an invading virus is *in* a body. The concept either precedes or is simultaneous with the construction of the word pattern, or else it is never present. But information is present at the end of the process, so it must be present at the start as well.

The relationship of the mind to the material and the immaterial aspects of the world is complex, in part, because not all mental objects are immaterial. Feelings, for example, are arguably material mental objects. But words embody concepts, and concepts are meanings that exist as universals and not as particular material things. This way of thinking about what a word is depends on the difference between natural signs and intentional relations. Natural signs exist because there is a cause and effect relation in nature: smoke is a sign of fire, fever is a sign of infection. But for a sign to be a symbol, intention is required. A "No Soliciting" placard is intended to deliver the message that soliciting is prohibited. "Oncology" means the field of medicine dedicated to treating patients with cancer. These formal relations cannot be understood in material terms. Rational arguments do not physically compel, and there is no shape that is the meaning of a word.

The meaning of a word is identical to the concept it conveys. While material things exist as particulars, concepts exist as universals. All concepts are mental objects that exist and are real, but they do not exist the way that material things exist, because they are immaterial things that exist only in people's minds. According to Aristotle, we do not understand a concept; rather, a concept is that by which we understand. Concepts are tools we use to understand the world in which we live. Our intellect abstracts a thing's form from its shape, turning observation into in*form*ation. The intellect is the faculty capable of grasping concepts, forms, or essences.

Words exist at the intersection of material and immaterial realms. They are physical things, but they are not merely physical. The relation between a word and its meaning is not a physical relation. A person who grasps the meaning of a word is active, whereas the word itself is passive. Something that acts must *be* before it can act. The intellect that grasps immaterial meaning is a necessary condition for understanding. Even if the physical body is the instrument by which the understanding becomes actual, when I understand something, my intellect is using my physical body—not vice versa. Even if the intellect cannot exist apart from the body, it must still be immaterial if it is rational: rational agency and free choice imply each other, and an intellect must transcend the laws of material nature or else its actions would be bound by physical laws of cause and effect. As far as we know, the brain is a necessary condition of rational thought in humans, and discoveries about the brain are consistent with the rest of science. But the laws of science cannot produce a sufficient account of human thought, because human thought deals with immaterial concepts that do not follow the laws of cause and effect needed for the scientific explanation of a thing. The rationality of science depends upon the immaterial nature of the mind, which transcends the very laws of nature that are the subject of scientific investigation and theorizing.

Words allow our concepts and ideas to be communicated to others, and the concepts embodied in words make it possible to order rationality. Words are material things that carry meanings, and they can bring about events in the world such as marrying someone or starting a revolution. The intellect does things with words. All brain states are either subject to efficient causes in the brain, ordered by the laws of nature and fully open to scientific investigation, or else they are ordered by the intentional acts of the intellect. Acts of the intellect that carry intention transcend the threshold of scientific investigation, because they are neither determined nor predictable. They are free. The intending intellect is capable of observing final causation in nature, but because it is free and immaterial, a material scientific instrument can detect neither final causality nor an intellect capable of grasping final causality.

This Aristotelian perspective need not be accepted in its entirety to think about philosophical imagination and the power of the poetic apriori in a meaningful universe. But the remainder of my discussion will lean on several ideas that emerge from an Aristotelian account—immaterial concepts, the relationship of meaning to words, and the ability of our intellects to abstract form from the shapes of things and to grasp immaterial meaning. The realm of meaning, freedom, and rationality is distinct from the world of determined material causation susceptible to investigation by the sciences. This distinction is crucial for understanding the role of the poetic apriori in philosophical imagination, as well as the central idea illuminating the nature of the imagination in a world that is meaningful as a whole—the analogia entis.

II. Imagination and Our Knowledge of Creation and God

The poetic apriori emerges from acts of philosophical imagination in minds disposed toward what Giambattista Vico called *sapienza poetica*—discovery of truth and significance through artifacts made by the imagination in a universe that is meaningful as a whole. Analogy is the structure undergirding the service of the poetic apriori in the work of philosophical imagination. Analogy is a solution to the problem of how an infinite and transcendent God can be named and explored, using names that originate in the immanent world of humans. God is all-in-all, and yet creation exists. The absolute is expressed in the immanent. We discover God in our naming, because the names of things in a created world are fundamentally analogical. All worldly being and worldly knowledge, including metaphysical knowledge, have analogical character because the God who is the form of form, the essence of essence, establishes all creaturely form and essence. God is the object of all suppositions of naming.

This is why metaphor is not merely a literary device but is constitutive of part of the mind's experience in a created world. It reveals cognitive structures, along with deep patterns of order in other parts of created reality. It orients us toward the world as meaningful and toward nature as created—as originating from, and grounded in, an act of God. In a created universe, imagination is not opposed to reason but instead works with reason to spy out meaning in the world. A connection grasped through metaphor—seeing *this* in *that*—is more than a superficial comparison. It provides insight into creation as a whole, which is to say the universe as a cosmos.

Because our knowledge is always provisional, one function of the imagination is to frame and explore the possible meanings of a thing, a fact, or an event. For Thomas Aquinas, imagination makes other forms of knowing possible for us. He says that the human intellect cannot grasp unveiled universal truth, because its nature requires it to be understood by turning to the phantasms.[6] Human contemplation requires the imagination, but through imagination we can contemplate the purity of intelligible

---

[6] Aquinas, *Summa Theologica* I q3 a1; q84, a7. [Throughout this book, citations of the *Summa Theologica*—including volume, question, and article—are from Thomas Aquinas, *Summa Theologica*, trans. Fathers of the English Dominican Province, Benziger Bros., New York, NY (1981).]

truth.⁷ Imagination's discovery of reality involves a practical exercise in learning to see the radiance of things that are perfect insofar as they are actual.⁸ The power that allows us to see this radiance through imagination is derived from a higher intellect: the intellectual light in our souls comes from God.⁹

The relationship of the imagination to the soul and body is central to Thomas's theological anthropology. In the body, we come to know the things of the world through the imagination. But there is also a role for images as we begin to know God, including the dim likeness to God within humans: "The image of God exists in man as in an alien nature, as the image of the King is in the coin."¹⁰ God as the exemplar infinitely exceeds the likeness within us. But the image of God is more perfect in humans than in angels, because whole human soul is in the whole human body, and God has an analogous relation to the whole world. The Trinity is found in the acts of the human soul. From the knowledge that we possess, we form an internal word (a kind of naming) through thought, and this breaks forth into love. Analogy is the path to knowledge of God's causes, because God is the creator of the harmony in the universe. It shows us how causality functions among parts of the whole and the ways in which the whole leads our minds toward the cause of everything. The different parts of reality are linked by knowledge we discover through analogy.

In a created universe of the sort Thomas inhabits, the imagination's relationship to the world is inseparable from the idea that we are made the image of God. A vision of glory allows the temporal things in creation to be seen as originating with God, and we are able to have this vision because we are made in the image of God.¹¹ An imperfect happiness is possible for anyone in this life, though only the vision of God can bring about perfect happiness. The speculative and practical uses of intellect that constitute happiness in this life are dependent upon imagination. The imagination is a storehouse for the phantasms it generates in its mediation between a thing and its concept. Phantasms—the mind's images of extramental realities outside the senses—reside in the body.¹² But the divine

---

[7] Aquinas, *Summa Theologica* 2-2 q180, a5.
[8] Aquinas, *Summa Theologica* I-II q3, a2.
[9] Aquinas, *Summa Theologica* I q79, a4.
[10] Aquinas, *Summa Theologica* I q93, a1.
[11] Aquinas, *Summa Theologica* I q3, a8.
[12] Aquinas, *Summa Theologica* I q84, aa6,7.

essence cannot be seen by means of a phantasm.[13] This means the body is not needed for the happiness that consists in a vision of divine essence, though such vision is transformative for the full human experience of temporal creation. Within this transformed universe of temporal and created things, we find joy in comparing one thing with another, because comparison of one thing with another is part of our nature.[14] Imagination allows us to grasp analogical and metaphorical correspondences, and to pray in accordance with the truth of nature.

We experience nature through our senses, either directly or through the instrumental extension of our senses in experimentation. If the world is created, the meaning of creation can only be explored in light of the creator. Natural theology of this sort lights up the world and leads to joy in experience, because there is no idea of a *thing* that is not in some way related the idea of *God*. This is why Nicholas of Cusa believed that we taste eternal wisdom in everything that can be tasted, because it is itself the beauty in everything beautiful and the desire in everything for which we long.[15] For a theist, there is a fragrance of eternal wisdom in every part of creation. Daily life becomes a philosophical adventure and an act of worship that enlivens, and is enlivened by, imagination's reach toward what is not yet fully known or seen.

We name the things we find in the world, and we long for the name of God. Our naming and our longing are always from inside our created human nature, including our understanding of the name of God. We want to understand interconnections among apparently disparate things, and we want to understand the meaning of things. Imagination explores as-yet vaguely grasped meanings, and it expresses these through argument, poetry, music, fiction, visual arts, liturgy, and scientific theories. When we make stories about the world, we are trying to show something of the light we have seen. The making itself is part of the light, part of the adventure of discovery.

Imagination changes our conscious experience of the world. Because we are limited creatures, there are things we cannot yet consciously experience. But everything that can be consciously experienced can be imag-

---

[13] Aquinas, *Summa Theologica* I q12, a3.
[14] Aquinas, *Summa Theologica* I-II q32 a8.
[15] Hans Urs von Balthasar, *The Glory of the Lord: A Theological Aesthetics, V, The Realm of Metaphysics in the Modern Age*, trans. Oliver Davies, Andrew Louth, Brian McMeil, John Saward, and Rowan Williams, Ignatius Press, California (1991), 228.

ined. This is how the imagination grows. And as imagination grows, conscious perception of reality grows. Imagination stretches into reality, and our ever-expanding conscious experience follows. In a created universe, the possibilities for such a faculty are infinite. But the imagination requires the intellect to discern truth since the imagination deals with what is possible, but not everything that is possible exists. This is one of the mysteries of imagination and its relationship to the conundrums of existence: possibilities are real even when they do not exist. Imagination shows us that reality is not exhausted by existence, which is why we need humility, however optimistic our epistemology might be.

What we experience inwardly though contemplation, prayer, and thought, we express outwardly in painting, music, writing, and anything else we make to appeal to the minds of others. For people of faith, Scripture is a uniquely important reservoir of imaginative expression. The images in Scripture can move the heart toward a hope, goal, act, or disposition. Where we experience spiritual darkness as veil or pall, clarity can emerge. The images can lead to repentance. They can orient us toward the beauty and truth of creation, and they can reveal the source of transformative and benevolent power. Scriptural images can become portals into mystery and hope. Analogy moves us beyond the world as it appears to our senses. Scriptural images are analogical in this sense, pointing toward a reality that cannot be contained within an image. This approach to Scripture shapes how we think about biblical accounts of prayer and sacrifice, including horrific sacrifices reminding us that we owe our lives to God. Abraham was told to sacrifice his only son Isaac, and Hosea was told to take a wife of whoredom and have children of whoredom because the land committed whoredom by forsaking the Lord. To see the images as anything other than analogical is to commit idolatry. In Scripture, images of faith hover between revelation and idolatry. Prophets serve to help us see the images for what they are so that we avoid idolatry without dismissing the good unveiled through the images. But when images have their proper place, they can correct our perceptions of creation so that we do not transform science, philosophy, or theology into idolatry of a different kind, mistaking shadows for reality without remainder. If we are aware of the spiritual trap of idolatry, we can discover the true value of scriptural images and analogy for grasping the deep radiance of creation.

We begin with sensible effects experienced in creation. Through analogical imagination we ascend to knowledge of the transcendent, including knowledge that God is the first cause, rather than one of the effects of creation. We come to know about God's infinity, and from this we learn about God's omnipresence. We come to know both God's transcendence and God's immanence in created things. These names for God's characteristics fundamentally depend on analogy as part of the solution to how our experience of this finite and imminent creation, from which we derive all names, can meaningfully refer to the transcendent. We must think about God without making God another thing among things in the universe. The power of analogical imagination depends upon the metaphysical idea that the world is intelligible because of its relation to its divine origin.

We use language to conceive of reality and to express what we find of reality. We know how to use the word "blue" to talk about the color blue. But once we begin to analyze the relationship between the unity of a thing and its name, as Ludwig Wittgenstein taught us, we see how difficult it is to keep a thing and its name together. This is especially true for names we attribute to God. Because our minds evolved within a universe of determinate objects, the idea that God is not a being among beings is difficult to grasp. The analogia entis provides a philosophical frame for exploring this concept of God. It does so in a way that also leads to discoveries about our own created natures. Because we are made in the image of God, our imaginations and intellects confront clues about God as we grow in understanding of ourselves and of the ways we experience the universe in which we exist. We are changed by discoveries that clarify themselves through our attempts to say or show what we have found.

When we use analogy to hold things together in our minds—things that somehow also hold together in reality—we are borrowing words about one kind of thing and using them to talk about another kind of thing. Within creation, analogy opens our minds to relationships among finite things. But when we use analogy to imagine God, we are reaching from the sphere of the immanent to that of the transcendent, from the finite to the infinite. We are pointing to an effect in the created world and reaching for a cause that is different from other causes within creation, but that must also be the same in some way. The scientific imagination can move from the appearance of experimental phenomena to theories about relations that hold in a quantum world to which we have no direct access. The philosophical imagination moves in a comparable way. In the case of scientific imagination, there are many layers of theory between the squiggle that registers scatter-patterns of energy on the monitor and the conclusions about what reality lies beneath the phenomenon. Likewise, the speculative enterprise of philosophical imagination in a created world begins with effects in the world and then reaches for the unseen reality that is the source of intellectual and imaginative light enabling us to see the significance of things that appear in the world. Our imaginations and intellects must be trained to be able to see the world lit up in this way. It is a light to which we can certainly close our eyes.

The creator's light casts shadows across the surface of the world. We learn about both God and creation by the way things mingle with God's light. To my ear, Austin Farrar is describing the analogia entis when he writes, "Perhaps our awareness of the infinite Act depends on the materials for a shadow of them presented by finite existence."[16] Such a metaphor provokes us to ask about the reality revealed through the shadow, rather than merely measuring the dimensions and gradations of light and gray in the shadow itself. For a philosophical imagination open to possibilities in a created universe, the figure of the shadow is the figure of everything that shows up in the cosmos. If the Apostle Paul is right that in God we live and move and have our being, our entire existence is lived in the shadow of God. There is no inside or outside to the shadow. There is only the inward shift of the one who perceives the shadow, and who sees, or fails to see, its significance. Seeing is always seeing *as*. If we want to perceive existence rightly, we must learn the deep structures of existence, the calculus of being. We must become the kind of people who can see. There is no end to the variety of what shows up and no end to the conversion of our imaginations and intellects as we grow into the act of seeing *as*. The poetic apriori is grounded in this experience of conversion, a kind of baptism of the imagination.

We can learn to contemplate luminous things. As we do, metaphysical reality registers in our minds as pleasure. This pleasure is kin to ecstasy, because it is the imprint of the very great in the very small, of heaven's truth in the human mind, of tracks left in the imagination by a passing presence. The smallest leaf can be the crack in the dam through which the joy of this experience seeps. The joy can also come through contemplative focus on an idea, such as Anselm's ontological proof for the existence of God, suddenly lighting up the mind. In either case, the living form playing in the theater of the philosophical mind awakens us to something that is not ourselves, something that helps us become better witnesses in a strange universe. Our minds grow past the pursuit of familiar distractions and the universe becomes less strange as the distensible gift of the

---

[16] Austin Farrar, *The Glass of Vision*, Glasgow University Press, Glasgow (1948), 84.

imagination locks onto the abundant clues pointing beyond the gaudy, frill-draped world that would have us pass time to keep us from noticing that time is passing. Delight beckons to us from everywhere.

Adam Zagajewski wrote a wonderful little poem that is just such a moment of noticing:

Auto Mirror

In the rear-view mirror suddenly
I saw the bulk of the Beauvais Cathedral;
great things dwell in small ones
for a moment[17]

In one sense, anyone who looks in that rear-view mirror can see the Beauvais Cathedral. But not everyone will look. Among those who glance not everyone will see the cathedral, perhaps because they were deciding whether or not there was room for a lane change. Among those who notice the cathedral, not everyone will make the leap to the insight that Zagajewski had, seeing great things dwell in small ones for a moment. Our minds need a contemplative pause to register the image in this way, or to allow our imaginative lives to be stretched by the poem, this small thing within which a great thing dwells for a moment. The same is true for our experience of the cathedral itself. Some people will see no more than a big incomplete building that was started in 1225, demonstrating innovations in Gothic architecture while embroiled in the usual financial and political struggles that accompany so many substantial human endeavors. But others will see the cathedral as another small thing within which a greatness dwells for the moment, before it is turned back into dust by time or war. Seeing of this sort requires a kind of faith. Faith is how the imagination sees the structures of transcendence in things so small as a poem, a cathedral, or any other created being.

The experience of God is another example of something that must be believed to be seen. The same experiences interpreted as encounters with God by theists can be interpreted in a naturalistic or humanistic way by non-theists. Things occur in the imagination of the one who sees with faith, which cannot occur in the imagination of one who does not see with faith, simply because the faith and the seeing are the same thing. We would not criticize a blind person for not seeing the cathedral, nor would we criticize

---

[17] Adam Zagajewski, „Auto Mirror" in *A Book of Luminous Things*, ed. Czeslaw Milosz, Harcourt, New York (1996), 128.

a person incapable of doing mathematics for not seeing the beauty of the calculations needed to construct a cathedral that does not fall under its own weight. But on the other hand, what if we believe we see something that is not actually there? Though blindness can prevent a person from seeing what is clearly there for someone with eyes to see, delusion can make a person see something a non-delusional person will not see, because it does not exist. How does the deluded person move beyond delusion, and how does the blind person move beyond blindness? All of us can hope for new ways of seeing, whether through the healing of damaged eyes, as with the blind, or through teaching, as with the beauty of mathematics. We can reach into the experience of other minds using the tools of the imagination. Images, stories, arguments, and poetry made by one person can teach another person to see differently. But can we deepen our apprehension of reality through creative expansion of the imagination?

Anselm provided a profound thought experiment to answer this question. He wanted to construct a single argument for the existence of God, and this led him to prescribe an imaginative act that he claimed was ontologically revealing. In the *Monologion* he had created a series of arguments to show how through reason alone, one can discover that God exists, that God is omnipotent, that God is the creator of everything that exists, and so forth. But this was an unsatisfying approach, because it required independent arguments for God's existence and for each of God's characteristics. Anselm wanted a single, elegant argument that would do the work of all the separate arguments he constructed in the *Monologion*. He did not doubt the chained-together arguments he made, but he did not like their complexity. He wanted one argument that would do it all, a master argument. According to stories about Anselm, he became obsessed with this philosophical preoccupation. He lost sleep over it, and he found himself unable to concentrate in church, which is an occupational liability for a monk. But eventually he hit upon the argument. Because of Immanuel Kant, it has become known as the ontological argument for the existence of God, even though Kant was not familiar with Anselm. Medieval thinkers simply called it *Anselm's argument*. He made the argument in the *Proslogion*. If it works, it demonstrates the existence of God, as well as the various characteristics of God.

Anselm's guiding motto was *faith seeking understanding*. He thought of faith as a love for God leading to a desire for deeper knowledge of God. Because Anselm wrote for other monks, he was not primarily concerned with belief in God. Nonetheless, he constructed the argument in such a way that even non-theists would be convinced of the existence of God if they truly understood it. Because his devoted search for this master argument began to seem perilously similar to a temptation, he tried to stop thinking about it. One day during Matins, when his mind was wandering back to the argument, he suddenly saw it.

This is what he saw: *God is that than which nothing greater can be thought*. Anyone willing to do the necessary imaginative work can grasp this idea, regardless of his or her faith or lack of faith. The definition simply refers to a being that is so great that a greater being cannot even be conceived. Once the idea is conceived, that than which nothing greater can be thought exists in the understanding. This means it must also exist in reality, because something that exists in reality is greater than something that exists only in understanding. If that than which nothing greater can be thought only exists in understanding, then it is not that than which nothing greater can be thought, because we can imagine it existing in reality. This is a contradiction. The only way to escape the contradiction is to see that that than which nothing greater can be thought actually exists. And this is God.

Little time passed before critics responded to Anselm's argument. The most famous early criticism came from another monk named Gaunilo, in a piece he called *Reply on behalf of the fool* (since one target of Anselm's argument was the fool who, according to the psalmist, says in his heart that there is no God). Gaunilo offered an alternative imaginative experiment. Instead of imagining that than which nothing greater can be thought, try to imagine that island than which no greater can be thought. Once we have grasped this idea, it exists in our understanding. But, by Anselm's reasoning it must also exist in reality, because the island existing in reality is greater than the island existing only in our understanding. If it does not exist, we have the same contradiction: that island than which no greater can be thought is not that island than which no greater can be thought. But it is ridiculous to believe that such an island actually exists. For the same reason, Anselm's argument for the existence of God fails— or at least the argument as Gaunilo conceived it fails.

How did Anselm answer Gaunilo? He said the argument works for God but not for the island. Unfortunately, in his reply he did not say why it works for God but not for the island. Instead, he offered a clearer exposition of his original argument. He thought Gaunilo raised two important points. First, Gaunilo objected to the existence in our understanding of that than which nothing greater can be thought—we cannot form the idea required to get the argument going. Second, even if we can form the idea of God as that than which nothing greater can be thought, there is nothing in the idea that guarantees God's existence. Anselm's clarification of his own argument depended on showing, first, that the idea of that than which nothing greater can be thought can actually be thought, and second, that thinking this thought will lead one to just see that it must exist in reality. This is why it is an ontologically revealing imaginative act.

What are we doing when we think of God? We are either thinking of something that exists, or thinking of something that might exist but probably does not, or thinking of a purely imaginary thing that does not exist. We can bring each of these possibilities into our minds and examine them. But we cannot bring something that is impossible into our minds. We cannot bring a round square into the gaze of our thought. Anselm's point is this: that than which nothing greater can be thought cannot be thought not to exist. To think of that than which nothing greater can be thought as not existing, is to think an impossible contradiction, and this the mind cannot do. If you attempt to think of that than which nothing greater can be thought, but you think of it as not existing, you have not yet actually grasped the thought. It is a very difficult thought to achieve, and those who deny the existence of God have simply not yet had the thought. Furthermore, there is no other thought like this thought. Other thoughts might vaguely take the form of this thought, but they are not actually like this thought, because there is nothing that can be compared to God. The move that Gaunilo made was to use something less than God to address an argument that is about something utterly different, higher, and singular—namely, God.

What about the second point? God has no beginning, because a being with no beginning is greater than one that begins to exist. If we do the work required to think that than which nothing greater can be thought, we must think of God as a possible being. We cannot think of God as beginning to exist, because that is to think of a possible being that is not that than which nothing greater can be thought, and so we are not thinking of God. That than which nothing greater can be thought, therefore, is a necessary being. One who does not see this has not yet grasped that than which nothing greater can be thought. All Anselm meant to claim was that if you are thinking of that than which nothing greater can be thought as not existing, you have not yet thought the thought. Keep trying.

The *Proslogion* is offered as a prayer. The prayer produces a change in a mind. It moves the mind to sift through images and words until it comes to the threshold of something that we either see or fail to see. Even if we have not yet seen it, we still have to decide whether or not to believe that Anselm saw it. Criticisms such as Gaunilo's might seem initially persuasive, but Anselm talks past Gaunilo's objections and provokes us to try again. The work is imaginative and contemplative. In this, it is similar to the work required to grasp Leibniz's central philosophical question, *Why is there something rather than nothing?* Theories that locate the beginning of the universe in conditions called "nothing," but that nonetheless use metaphors of vacuums, laws, and other force-like entities, fail to acknowledge how difficult it is to truly imagine nothing. By nothing, Leibniz meant *nothing*—no space, no vacuum, no laws, no forces. Nothing. Getting to the actual thought of nothing is imaginatively difficult. But, as I mentioned at the beginning of this book, once we achieve the idea of nothing, we just see the power of Leibniz's question as we imagine something—anything—and then imagine this something coming from nothing. Anselm's argument requires the same kind of work.

This kind of seeing is not merely an imaginative act of mind. Anselm thought it revealed something important about who God is. This is faith seeking understanding. Once Anselm saw his great argument, he responded with worship. If we are able to see what Anselm would have us see, our imaginative organization of reality will change. The complete reality of God is not contained in the idea, but rather the world is opened up and illuminated once this insight alters the mind. A mind changed in this way becomes aware of unspeakable reality, and the change also compels us to make something out of words, musical notes, colors, or bodily movements as we try to say what cannot be said. This resonates with Plato's allegory of the cave, in which the philosopher returns to the darkness of the cave to share a glimmer of what is real, using tools that are not themselves the reality but a means of provoking, changing, shaping, and growing the imaginations of others for whom reality is limited to familiar shadows on the wall.

The imagination is a symbolizing power that draws on the structural force of analogy. At one level analogy shows what is similar among disparate things. But at a deeper level, closer to the threshold of what is most primordial—the ultimate *apriori*—it reveals an utterly different reality, for which we do not have adequate language. Such an act of imagination is not only a refinement of the vision natural to us but also a conversion to possibilities that first show up as glimmers and echoes in the hidden parts of our minds, a radically vast expansion on the idea of re-membering.

When we have an idea in our mind, that idea is the meaning of the words we use to show it to another mind. Words do not comprehensively contain the idea present to our mind. But our words (or other ways of saying a thing) nonetheless evoke the fullness of the thing in other minds. Words have the power to show us how to see what we would not otherwise have seen, to be receptive to reality in ways we might not otherwise have been. Anselm wanted to show what is accessible to reason without revelation. That is a severe restraint, if imagination is leading the mind toward a God who is incomprehensible by reason. Once a poet or philosopher grasps that toward which Anselm's argument gestures, they must draw on something more than philosophy and poetry to go deeper into the reality they have glimpsed. This is where the prophet comes on the stage.

The prophet's acts are different than the imaginative acts of the philosopher or the poet. Poetic and philosophical works can register patterns in existence that derive from a force transcending our existence. But prophecy claims to come from within the transcendent force itself, speaking into the very patterns of existence traced by the poets and the philosophers. If prophecy is sometimes also poetry, it is a very different kind of poetry and a very different use of the analogical bridge across the chasm between creation and creator. Jeremiah was a prophet-poet who, in Austin Farrar's description, "sets images moving by musical incantation, and allows them to arrange and express themselves as they *ought*." Farrar goes on to ask, "What are we to say about this *ought*? ... If it is not 'just life' which presses Jeremiah, then what is it that presses him, and constrains his images?"[18] The constraint on Jeremiah's images is nothing other than the will of God who impacts creation, history, and the prophet's own inspired mind. Jeremiah's work can only be understood in relation to the larger pattern of divine will that emerges through his words as he addresses the people of Israel, people who are inextricably bound to forces in a world that came from an eternal source through the act of creation. If we cannot imagine any force beyond the political and economic realities Israel encountered and rebelled against, we will not be able to hear Jeremiah's words as prophecy or great poetry. We can truly hear Jeremiah only if our imagination is shaped by faith.

---

[18] Farrar, *The Glass of Vision*, 125.

With enough intellectual and imaginative work, anyone can grasp Anselm's argument. But to go farther than seeing the existence and characteristics of a necessary being, faith seeking understanding must make leaps and take risks. We are fallible, and our stories about the world, even if they are inspired, are limited by the one through whom they come, the one who hears them, and cultural circumstances of the teller and the listener. Our stories, like our metaphysics, will always be creaturely, for what else could they be? That said, if we are open to the possibility of prophecy, faith seeking understanding must acknowledge the difference between what the poets and the prophets are doing. Poets make poems, using imagination to mold pieces taken from history, nature, and human experience. They show us new possibilities that we might play with and test to learn a novel way of seeing or thinking. But the true prophet does not make prophecy in the same sense. Prophets respond to the will of an eternal other, and they proclaim the demands of that will. They are not trying to evoke contemplation but to change action and to shape the character of a people in a way that conforms more deeply to the will of God. For the prophet, the inspired poem is merely one way in which a divine message is delivered. The metaphors and forms of the prophet's poems signal the fiery force of the Divine moving in the prophet's mind, pushing aside the prophet's own motives and thoughts.

Another way to say this is to acknowledge that every poet works under the pressure of some force—every poet has a muse. When Dante writes a love poem about Beatrice, he certainly borrows the words and syntax from the same Italian the cobbler uses, weaving dialects into an Italian that had never been heard before, but the force of his love for the young woman is his own, and we have no reason to doubt the substance of that force. In the same way, faith seeking understanding opens us to the poetry of a prophet, whose gift is to listen for the mysterious force of the divine, and it prepares us to be taught things that are beyond our own minds. But neither the words nor the syntax, which we use all day for other purposes of our own, contain the mystery of the prophet's poem. The force of the poem itself is not magic. The poem is not an incantation. It contains no power apart from the movement of the divine that inspires the prophet's mind.

The images created in Dante's imagination signified the force of his love for Beatrice, a love evoked by her alone. The images in the poems of a prophet are likewise evoked by the divine. They point beyond themselves, existing in service to the one who made the prophet's mind move in a particular way. Such images cannot be translated into metaphysical propositions without remainder. But because they point toward a reality beyond images and creaturely metaphysics, they bridge the gap between the reality of the God who moves the prophet's mind and the work of the devoted metaphysician who, in faith, is seeking to understand. Images from the inspired imagination of a prophet improve our metaphysics. Likewise, the work of philosophy prepares us to receive the reality toward which the prophet's images point. These acts of the imagination constitute one whole in the human mind at its best, and the mind is at its best when life is lived in the rhythm of the holy.

III. Imagination and the Holy

In a created universe, certain philosophical acts, such as the work of thinking Anselm's *that than which nothing greater can be thought*, are simultaneously acts of reason, imagination, and contemplative prayer. Thomas Kelly, a philosopher raised in a Quaker tradition, exemplified this in his life and thought. The mysticism that shaped his life, including the most mundane daily activities, reached toward reality through every portal available to the mind. This mysticism answered a deficit he perceived in modern psychology, which cannot account for sacred or secular flashes of insight. Insight comes as the creative mind of God bubbles up and expresses itself though the imaginations of people whose spirits have been prepared by the love of God, who woos us toward a life of holiness: "An increment of infinity is about us. Holy is imagination, the gateway of Reality into our hearts."[19]

Our understanding of the philosophical imagination depends upon our anthropology. Kelly embraced the analogical idea of a central holy place within us where we hear the voice of God, encounter light, and touch eternity. This inward reality shows us how to view God, the world, other people, and ourselves. It is the *Shekinah*, a sense of the presence of God, not in some ethereal nether-region reserved for a few prophets or saints—but inside all of us. It calls us to reorient ourselves toward deepest reality, even as we go about our daily tasks. Engaging with the divine does not lead us out of the world but instead lights up everything that is taken for granted, showing the true wonder of something as common as the face of a friend or a stranger. This requires humility. Because there is so much distraction in life, we have to practice to remain aware of the multiple orders and operations of the mind that register radiance in the world and in ourselves. This practice leads to a pervasive and joyful transformation.

A kind of holy play occurs at the level of mind where the transcendent and immanent meet, and we experience the presence of God. Out of this play come the mystic's metaphors and the philosopher's tools for reflective thought. The life of God, in which we are invited to share, is always new, creative, and energizing. We most fully live this reality through our commitments and acts of worship, not through our theories. Our theologies, doctrines, and creeds are useful, but they are also transient. If the

---

[19] Thomas Kelly, *Testament of Devotion*, HarperOne, New York (1996), 33.

universe is created, all being is oriented toward God, irrespective of the metaphors we use to express the meaning and purpose we discover in the world. The central reality of God's enlivening presence reaches across the surface differences of our cultures and makes us one. This is the always-present heavenly hum of reality, the light that changes the way we see and care about the world with all its mess and strife and beauty.

This light illuminates imagination, reality's gateway into our hearts. The light is not an incremental and laborious lure toward yet more tasks. It is a complete change in our vision of the world, leading to a new way of being, or to say something equally true, a new way of being that leads to a new way of seeing. This transformative change in our posture toward reality is most fully expressed in the word "worship." We become new creatures when we worship in this light. We are astonished by our spontaneous responses to the world and to other people that arise from the love of God, a love so deeply valuable that the world's greatest treasures appear drab by comparison. This change does not occur because of abstractions we chart on a map of knowledge. It occurs because we act in faithfulness to the goodness, truth, and beauty we have so far encountered.

We lose ourselves in the course of the journey. But as we empty ourselves, we will discover that we are filled with the presence of God, which introduces us to new experiences of happiness, serenity, and creativity. This is the fountain of creative Mind that wells up and expresses itself within prepared spirits; this is the root of the poetic apriori. The divine, infinite, and incomprehensible is beneath, within, and above reality. It is constitutive of reality. The imagination is the portal through which this reality enters our consciousness and surprises us with poetry that shapes the imaginations of others, artifacts that draw their minds toward their own discovery of this presence and how to participate in it.

Once we taste this presence and understand the role of imagination in our discovery of reality, we also learn that our imaginations are not our own. We share imagination with others, as their voices and ideas set up shop in our memories, shaping the philosophical lenses with which we see the world, each other, and ourselves. We are freed as we relinquish the illusion of the sharply inscribed boundaries that constitute our individual selves, rather than laboring to strengthen and protect them. We discover a new humility toward the frailty of our own self-originated intentions, because our true value rests upon the unmovable love and grace of God. Our experience of God's love corrects our sense of genuine worth in the world and in our lives: "Only the inner vision of God, only the God-blindness of unreservedly dedicated souls, only the utterly humble ones can bow and break the raging pride of a power-mad world."[20]

The virtues of patience, self-control, gentleness, and honesty grow within this lit-up serenity, the fruit of imaginative peace rather than laborious accomplishment. But a new acquaintance with suffering also arises. We see the struggles of other people more clearly, and growth in holy obedience leads us to engage with the world in all its sorrow and brokenness. Because suffering is everywhere, we must allow it into our imaginatively luminous world. We must reimagine suffering and our relation to it. Kelly's perspective on suffering was influenced by a conversation with a Hindu monk who taught him a secret paradox: *nothing matters, everything matters*. We must grasp this paradox if we want to understand suffering, to care for the suffering, and to allow ourselves to be cared for when we suffer. The paradox shows us what we can learn through suffering, and perhaps only through suffering. We learn to love and to be loved in a peculiar way in the middle of suffering.

If imagination is reality's holy gateway into our hearts, love is the true transparency that we lay on the world to see it well, meeting it in the moment. The act of love releases us from self-centeredness and from our burdensome efforts in the world. It allows us to become aware of the eternal, which is always breaking into our measured, urgency-filled time. In an eternity-brightened now, we come to know the divine as a fountain of love, a presence that is both the background of the cosmos and the condition for paying attention to the smallest life that shows up in our foreground. We learn to love and love again. By learning to love we learn to see, discovering the deep ontological homology between imaginative growth and the act of love.

As our imaginations grow, we learn more about divine presence in the act of love. We also learn the power of peace in our relation to the world and to others. We are pursued by love. This brings both peace and serenity. As our awareness of the *Shekinah* deepens, so does our faith that love can overcome anything in the world, including the grief of the sufferer. The converted imagination, grounded in faith, transforms seeing into a true act of love, which is a power much deeper than pity: "There is a tendering of the soul, toward *everything* in creation, from the sparrow's fall to the slave under the lash. The hard-lined face of a money-bitten financier is as deeply touching to the *tendered* soul as are the burned-out

---

[20] Kelly, *Testament of Devotion*, 37.

eyes of a miner's children, remote and unseen victims of his so-called success."[21]

Holiness, obedience, presence, and love are the deepest powers of philosophical imagination in a created universe. They lead to participation in the world, where our making is in harmony with reality. This is the poetic apriori. The phenomenologist, Edmund Husserl, glimpsed it in his idea that there is an enormous apriori in our minds, an inexhaustible infinity of apriori, and that through this, we approach the unapproachable. The mystics and the saints likewise have much to say about this apriori. Thomas Kelly was a witness to it. Occasionally, prophets of the imagination show up and remind us of the governing idea for the poetic apriori, the analogia entis. One such prophet was George MacDonald, a holy man who lived the fullness of the imagination in a created universe.

C. S. Lewis called George MacDonald his master. Lewis claimed that his own imagination was baptized when he first read MacDonald's book *Phantastes*. MacDonald was a novelist and a pastor committed to the work of tending souls. MacDonald read the world, human action, and the language of the mind from the perspective Kelly wrote about, infused with love and a sense of divine presence. He thought all words begin as poetry, originating in the imagination and populating the mind. But they grow dim and lose some of their poetic quality as they are put to common use with no mindfulness of their origins. What was once experienced as a symbol turns into a mere sign through forgetfulness. The imagination loses its responsiveness to the radiance of the created world and the mystery of naming in a world that is a gift: "Thus thousands of words which were originally poetic words owing their existence to the imagination, lose their vitality, and harden into mummies of prose. Not merely in literature does poetry come first, and prose afterwards, but poetry is the source of all language that belongs to the inner world, whether it be of passion or of metaphysics, of psychology or of aspiration."[22]

Nature matters in a peculiar and wonderful way for MacDonald, a way that is possible only if nature is created. The words that populate our minds clothe the things of the world. This reveals something about minds, words, and the world. We discover part of the truth of our own minds through the ways the world appears to us. By paying attention to the way our minds form words that connect to, and symbolize, the appearances, we

---

[21] Kelly, *Testament of Devotion,* 81.
[22] George MacDonald, *A Dish of Orts,* Forgotten Books, London (2012), 2.

also discover something about the truth of the world. This connection is not merely between facts and words as placeholders for facts (a bit of blue here referred to as *a bit of blue here*), but it also extends to feeling, giving metaphor its power as a poetic revelation of the true nature of minds and of the world. The imagination inhabits every form of thought. By persisting in mindful attentiveness, it seeks out the contours of the original divine imagination from which everything comes. From within this contemplative orientation toward the world as created, we see that the highest reality of a thing's form appears on its surface. All the depth of formal reality is discoverable by the imagination. The work of the intellect is to understand connections among forms on which the imagination shines its light. The harmony encountered in the play of forms on the surface of reality suggests to the intellect the operations of discoverable laws: "The poetic relations themselves in the phenomena may suggest to the imagination the law that rules its scientific life. Yea, more than this: we dare to claim for the true, childlike, humble imagination, such an inward oneness with the laws of the universe that it possesses in itself insight into the very nature of things."[23]

Francis Bacon believed that the excellent question is half of knowledge. MacDonald agreed, and he added that the source of the excellent question is the imagination. The imagination is the origin of any hypothesis that leads to discovery, because the imagination first glimpses the discoverable law, extending the reach of the intellect into new territory and shining light into areas that are as-yet dark to our understanding. When points of information appear in the world, the imagination apprehends the invisible connections that make a whole from the pieces. We must use the lenses of both science and imagination if we are going to reach into the darkness of ancient Earth, consolidating a story that allows us to move from the incompleteness of data to a vision of the whole connected with our present story.

MacDonald's robust sense of the world as created in love allows him to view the forms of nature as approximate representations of the human mind, not because the forms are imposed by our minds but because the outward material world is informed by immaterial thought, which also constitutes the gift of our minds: "The forms of nature are the representations of human thought by virtue of their being the embodiment of God's

---

[23] MacDonald, *Orts*, 7.

thought."[24] This makes nature readable by human beings. The exploration of nature's order and harmony is an exploration of the things of God. Our discovery is only partial and our imaginations must continue to reach. But the journey is filled with hope. When we discover harmony in one part of nature, our imaginations search for harmony in the rest of the cosmos, and the labor of science follows. Science grows because of its faith in the harmony of the whole, a faith that extrapolates from the harmony that we have already discovered. This faith, this hope, is a different order of human experience than our collection of mere facts. The imagination reveals the connection and harmony among reality's forms by gathering them around a higher thought that is itself revealed through the order of the artifacts the imagination creates. This is the central idea of the poetic apriori. The light of our minds, which derives from the creator of all life, allows our minds to reach into darkness, trusting not merely in the light we carry within us but also in the wisdom, truth, and beauty of an in-*form*-ed creation, which awaits our journey into its endless variety.

This faith provokes our continued imaginative reach and our sharing of discovery. It fills our experience with joy and hope along with terror and awe as we hold our candle in the dark, wondering what lies beyond the horizon. An imagination tuned to the divine order moves toward its highest end, which is a responsiveness to the harmony present in creation. As our imperfect imaginations align with the divine order of things, we learn to see beauty in even the most common task. Right imagination leads not only to a truer view of reality but also to a truer manner of service. The creator's love establishes the order of our minds in line with the grain of the universe, the wisdom and beauty of creation. Acts of the imagination that resonate with the divine are acts of love.

Thomas Kelly taught that obedience is central to the growth of the holy imagination as a portal of light. MacDonald likewise discovered that life educates the imagination, but we must live in accord with divine harmony if our growth is to continue. To grow into this divine harmony is to grow into harmony with our true nature. By relinquishing the concretions that accumulate in our lives and by losing what we call self, we enter the divine light that reveals our true selves. Our intellects and imaginations become truer by being good, which is not a matter of following some formula or creed but learning to see and to act in love. As we learn to love, our work reveals the harmony of creation in a clear and luminous way.

---

[24] MacDonald, *Orts*, 9.

Whether we write a great poem or provide a humble service to an ill friend, we overcome the dimness of a fog-strewn world. Artifacts of our imagination show forth the goodness of creation. That goodness shines through the windows of what we make in the world—faithfulness in love, a story, a piece of music, a system of laws, or a better way to cobble our neighbor's worn shoes. Light breaks into the world through all forms of making that arise from our experience of the *Shekinah*, bursting forth from every part of immanent creation.

MacDonald's enchanted understanding of the imagination contrasts with the views of philosophers who suggest that the universe is mostly dead, that what we call life is a transient anomaly on the face of mindless and purposeless matter, and that our minds are reducible to the same stuff—transient and accidental puffs sweeping across the otherwise inanimate, mindless, purposeless stuff of which the universe is made. This philosophical view has its own starting points and assumptions, like any other view. Some have argued that that science compels us to accept such a position, but that argument is probably incoherent because science arises from the very minds that disappear into purposeless matter: we would need a good reason to trust the output of such an accidental mass of molecules. For those of us who hold that there is more to the world, the position seems like a failure to penetrate to the inner sanctuary of life and meaning, refusing every indication that a deeper natural order gives a better account of the surfaces, of what appears in the world through our minds.

Embracing a starting point is always an act of faith. We are guided by what we believe the story of the whole to be. If the reality of minds, love, and the rest is a clue to a deeper reality, then poetry, history, philosophy, and science become holy inquiries. The ability to see the world in this way does not result from sterile attempts to believe a set of propositions. Rather, it follows from the whole of our lived experience, once we let go of the difficult-to-maintain belief that the *really real* is what remains when we dismantle all forms in the world of appearance. That is like tearing down a building until it is a pile of bricks and then insisting that only the bricks are really real, while the form of the building was an illusion created by the architect's mind. The growth of our ability to see reality depends on our honesty in handling the truth we already have: "Let the man who would rise to the height of his being, be persuaded to test the truth by the deed—the highest and only test that can be applied to the loftiest of all assertions. To every man I say, 'Do the truth you know, and you shall learn the truth you need to know.'"[25]

We want to know where we are, why we are here, and what we ought to do. The answers to these questions depend upon how we view the universe. If we are transient, accidental, purposeless aggregations of dead matter, our minds are anomalies in the universe, which, far from feeling like home, is a continual threat to the aberrant appearance of meaning-hungry minds in a meaningless world. But in a created universe, a mind is a very different thing. It is not an aberration that improbably showed up on the surface of dead matter. Instead, it is evidence of the deepest truth of the universe that lends glory to the world and to our images of the world. Our imaginations are at home as they reach in every direction—inward, outward, downward, upward. Love is the way into such a universe, love that is patient, forgiving, and all-embracing in its responsiveness to the unfamiliar, overcoming alienation and disorder with goodness: "We must wait patiently for the completion of God's great harmony, and meantime love everywhere and as we can."[26] Such a view of the universe is suffused with a profound hope.

This same hope became the ground of Charles Peguy's theological aesthetics, formed within a poetry that addressed humanity's condition with its sweeping trajectory of innocence, fall, and endurance of time leading toward death and redemption. Hope, rather than theoretical frames, governed the rhythm, pattern, and goal of his poetry. He did not philosophize abstractly, nor did he tarry moment by moment with the delight of seeing one sunset here, one cuckoo there. No, he created an entire poetic state for the actors in a drama of the human soul responding to the terrible strangeness of waking up to the reality of God and the reality of our own radical contingency—the reality that we are literally nothing, apart from this mysterious creator who is our source and sustenance.

On Peguy's poetic stage the driving force is hope, and the terror of our situation is utterly subsumed by the reality of love. Reciprocity is at the heart of this love. Far from being some self-subsistent transcendent reality in a lonely universe, God's word and God's being have been entrusted to creation in a way that allows people to respond in love. God also risks the possibility that we will not respond in love, but without this risk,

---

[25] MacDonald, *Orts*, 43.
[26] MacDonald, *Orts*, 127.

everything would be in vain. There are no transcendent verities or eternal powers that can remove the risk inherent in God's creation of a genuine possibility for love. There is only hope.

Central to Peguy's poetry is the image of the heart that beats and throbs with love for the fallen, sleeping, dull beloved. Risk and terror are part of the true nature of love. We can experience love's disconsolation, once we realize that safety and preservation are not the ends God seeks for us. God prods us toward deeper adventures in creation by nurturing true freedom, the condition for the reality of love. Terror is genuine terror in Peguy's theater, but it is transformed into hope by the awakening of love, with all its disorienting and risky freedom. His great poem, *The Portal of the Mystery of Hope*, begins, "The faith that I love the best, says God, is hope."[27]

Every day is a drama with a beginning, a middle, and an end. The beginning is the surprise of waking up, and the end is the curtain falling on the drama so that we can renew the strength spent in the day. It is unclear whether the drama of the day interrupts the repose of night or if falling into sleep interrupts the work, images, and adventures of the day. Night is the reservoir from which children draw strength, replenishing what they gave during the day and preparing them for the next joyful dive into the gift of life. Night is an abyss, but insofar as it renews, it is an abyss of grace. The reason for drawing strength from the night is to play in the day. Of course, the drama of the day is not always play, and night, as St. John of the Cross taught us, is not always repose for the soul. Our control over both is negligible. We fall into sleep. We awaken and cannot sleep any more. Day and night interrupt each other, but they are also necessary for each other. Hope gives us the sense that we can safely fall into sleep, knowing that night is not the end of the story, and it allows us to walk into the risks of love, work, and play when we awaken. At a cosmic level, Peguy's images of interruption are more complex, as all of creation is portrayed as a kind of interruption of God's eternity but an interruption that is invited, because it is the creation of God.

Invitation is a form of speech that is meant to be heard. Rather than focusing on abstract truth, Peguy's poetry focuses on speech among people. Invitation can come in forms other than words. Beauty speaks to us through a thing's completed form, but it also speaks to us when something is only on its way toward being fully formed. Beauty, like truth, is not an

---

[27] Charles Peguy, *The Portal of the Mystery of Hope*, trans. David Louis Schindler, Jr. and William B. Eerdmans, Michigan (1996), 3.

abstraction separated from our daily lives but appears through our creative acts. Making art is an act of worship. The aesthetic is rooted entirely in the religious for Peguy, but he has a broad concept of religious art, which is an act of worship. Art as worship is religious, not in terms of its explicit content or form but in the Catholic sense that to speak truly about reality is to speak religiously about it. The music erupting on Earth can transport the faith-formed imagination to the sounds and experiences of heaven. The phrases, notes, forms, and harmony are fully human, but because humans are created, even the meager offerings of the frail singers in worn robes become a portal for grace. From a religious perspective, such imperfect music points toward a divine hope, however incompletely it is expressed in our songs and poems.

Peguy reserves his most vigorous and searing wit for the forces that denigrate the imperfect budding of radiance for the sake of expedience. He derides efforts to make humans more productive and more useful to a commercial world that morphs our finitude into a transient contribution to the avaricious cataloging of profit. But his derision arises from his tender attention to the living heart that risks itself in singing its small song. He prefers the off-key ogle of a faithful heart calling out to God in response to the invitation of beauty, rather than the desiccating effects of commodity-driven economics that abstract the person from the community. Though Peguy is a thoroughly Catholic poet, he generalizes his points about religious art to all art expressing something religious in the human heart. He often expresses this through the children who show up in his poetry, not as an idolatrous framing of childhood but as a glimpse into the ways that play can teach us how to lose our false selves and learn to worship. Play resists mere utility that is deaf to song, blind to beauty, and cold to the tragedy of eliding the only portal for love and consciousness in this world—the mortal person.

Peguy sought to remedy the sickness of endless consumption by renewing the deep but faltering relationship between faith and culture. This relationship was the foundation of his understanding of religious art. The stakes could not be higher. Our terror of death's mystery, our obsession with money, and our labor to avoid risk and uncertainty diminish our ability to love well. They distract us from the adventure of living in the strange and wonderful gift of God's creation. Our worry drives us to become obsessed with the future, while our present slips into the past without our notice. Hans Urs von Balthasar described this risk-averse modern world as, "a monstrous old people's home, and institution for pensioners. The glorious insecurity of the present is always sacrificed to the security of the moment immediately following."[28]

We lose so much when imagination is made to serve powers that discard people for the sake of concepts and commodities. But the religious imagination has hope in the middle of such sadness. This hope is expressed in the seriousness of play. Play is a political activity for the imagination, resisting the efficiencies of the concentration camp and dispelling market coopts of the world's inherently superfluous beauty. The journey is full of risk, but the risk is the condition for all love, whether it is erotic love for another person or the love that drives us toward God—two forms of love that are in no way at odds with each other. Socrates taught that erotic love is central to our search for the divine, but one of the most sustained portrayals of erotic love leading to a deeper love for God is Dante's *The Divine Comedy*—an imaginative adventure that recapitulates the arc of conversion and the full engagement of imagination in a created world.

---

[28] Hans Urs von Balthasar, *The Glory of the Lord: A Theological Aesthetics, III, Studies in Theological Style: Lay Styles*, trans. Oliver Davies, Andrew Louth, Brian McMeil, John Saward, and Rowan Williams, Ignatius Press, California (1986), 477–78.

IV. Imagination and Love

Aristotle thought our intellect only knows what we perceive through our senses and what we reach through the imagination. When we contemplate the transcendent divine order, which is the most valuable of human acts, we do so by a divine aspect of intellect that does not belong to us by virtue of our human nature. Aquinas agreed that contemplation of divine things most deeply characterizes human beings, but he thought the intellectual and moral efforts of philosophy are simply part of the knowledge that occurs in the natural order.[29] Dante is closer to Aristotle on this point, though the basis for his position is quite different: the contemplative life requires transcendent revelation of divine reality, rather than being merely a natural human act. When Dante converted the platonic forms into the pure intelligences of angels, the starting points of Western philosophy were subsumed into contemplative intelligences that we cannot know through our senses and only through faith. The poetic challenge was to discover images that evoked such ideas.

We can reject or affirm the value of images in our exploration of divine reality. Dionysius the Areopagite chose the way of rejection, renouncing all images other than the final image in God. Dante chose the way of affirmation. He believed images bring us to God though a kind of analogical work in which they reveal the differences between God and creation but also illuminate the likenesses that transform our understanding of both. Like Thomas, he was filled with wonder before the incomprehensibility of God, and he understood the humility at the heart of the *via negativa*. St. Bonaventure, writing around the same time as Dante, said that God is a circle whose center is everywhere and whose circumference is nowhere.[30] Intellectual images of this sort suffuse Dante's poem, bringing together the way of affirmation and the way of rejection.

Whatever the poem's philosophical frame for knowledge might be, Dante was motivated by the image of Beatrice, a real woman who died and left him bereft. He experienced a moment of seeing eternity through her image. She communicated both love and humility, to the extent that Dante was able to receive them. She gave him knowledge of love that sprang

---

[29] Aquinas, *Summa Theologica* IaIIae, q3, a5, resp.

[30] Many have borrowed this description of God. It originates in the *Liber XXIV philosophorum,* attributed to the mythical figure Hermes Trismegistus, in which 24 philosophers come together, each giving a definition of God.

from, and revealed, a deeper well of love. Many of us occasionally experience this in our love for a few people, but if we were able to see better, we would find a glimpse of this deeper reality in every person. Dante's poem portrays what most of us experience in a confused way. We glimpse the eternal, but we become attached to the portal of glory and misplace our veneration, which leads to the distortions imagined in the *Inferno*.

After death took away the locus of Dante's ecstasy so that she was accessible only through imagination, he looked for consolation in philosophy, which transiently relieved him of his obsession. His turn to philosophy was an important choice of remedies, because it too was grounded in love—not only philia, the love fitting to friendship but also eros, which Socrates claimed was the kind of love that drove him toward wisdom. Dante was not the first man to fall in love with philosophy as a way to relieve the pain of heartbreak, nor was he the last. In his canzone, *Voi che 'ntendo il terzo ciel novete*, he sang about philosophy—the daughter of God, the queen of the universe.[31] This Lady, whose home is the divine mind, is a true friend to journeyers like Dante. For a time, he directed the fire of his passion toward this wonder-filled world of philosophical imagination that illuminated both visible and invisible things. He came to see that wisdom and love in the act of philosophical speculation are one with the faculty of imagination. But this was not enough, and eventually Dante was compelled to write his great poem. By the time he did so, he had concluded that the arts exist primarily to help the soul move more rapidly toward heaven.

Aquinas taught that love determines a person's share in the light of glory, because great love is accompanied by great desire, and desire prepares us to receive the one who is desired: "The greater a man's charity, the more perfectly will he see God."[32] Such love transforms the way we see and the way we imagine. Apart from Dante's great imaginative act of love in the *Divine Comedy*, Beatrice would have been remembered by others merely as a young woman from Florence who met Dante a couple of times, who became the second wife of Simone dei Bardi, and who died in June, 1290. But Dante was a witness to a different part of her truth, because he desired her and saw her with the eyes of love. From their dim, unlikely encounter on a small street in Florence, he realized that the key to grasping

---

[31] Dante Alighieri, *Il Convivio (The Banquet)*, trans. Richard H. Lansing, Garland Library of Medieval Literature, Ser. B. N (1990).

[32] Aquinas, *Summa Theologica* I, 12, 6, resp.

the whole of reality is love, and his imagination explored the massive cavern of treasure lit up by that love. Beatrice's transfiguration was not wrought by mere imagination; it was wrought by imagination shaped by faith. Dante was a Christian, and his spiritual and intellectual community included the dead. He did not treat this aspect of the universe as fiction. Beatrice—along with the others who populate the poem—continued to exist on the other side of death, even as he wrote his poem in Florence, daily walking past the Chapel of Santa Margherita de Cerchi. To read the poem well, our imaginations must be open to the same possibilities to which Dante's imagination was open, including the possibility of experiencing a love so great that it requires all of Earth, hell, purgatory, and heaven, along with the treasures of philosophy, poetry, and theology, to express itself.

Dante began his poem on the threshold of hell with images of savage forces, both inside and outside himself—the leopard of lechery, the ravenous lion of manhood, and a horrid *She* who always craves. These images drove him into his own dark past of treachery. His guide, Virgil, served as an image for both poetry and philosophy, an image of all human learning. But neither poetry nor philosophy were sufficient to answer the chaotic powers Dante met in the forest before passing through the gate into the inferno. When Dante and Virgil passed into hell they witnessed images of disordered affirmations, frozen into patterns forever fixed beyond the power of intellect and will to change—images of the petrified consciousness in an unchanging infinity.

Dante's poetic imagination lit up the grayness of the gloom in the *Inferno*, and revealed hell as a work of art that is as old as the world itself, constructed with the same wisdom and goodness God used to create heaven and earth.[33] Hell's impoverished version of love is neither nimble nor responsive. It is fixed and static, and the only form it takes is a singular kind of justice—punishment. God's love shows up only as punitive justice, and beauty shows up only in the symmetry and proportion between a sin and its punishment.[34] But it is there, because all communication requires at least a diminished act of love. As Dante and Virgil descended the funnel of hell, the character of that stunted, abbreviated communication is reified. This mirthless glimmer of form in the gloom of hell began with the episode

---

[33] Dante Alighieri, *The Divine Comedy*, trans. John Ciardi, W.W. Norton, New York (1970), 10–12.

[34] Hans Urs von Balthasar, *The Glory of the Lord: A Theological Aesthetics, III, Studies in Theological Style: Lay Styles*, Ignatius Press, California (1986), 91.

of Paulo and Francesca, right after what Charles Williams calls the Limbo of the suspended imagination.

Paulo and Francesca were lovers who committed adultery. At least, that is how the sin reads on the tablets of the Ten Commandments. The deeper truth of their sin was that they did not embrace the glory of the kind of love into which we are meant to grow. The elements of their love were good in themselves, but the goodness was not preserved. Their act led to disintegration. Their punishment occurs at the top of the funnel that is hell, and like all of the punishments in hell, the only change is the movement of infinite duration: all sins move toward the sameness of eternal fixity. The sin is sterile. It produces no fruit, no spiritual growth. Dante's images show sin for what it is, including its eternal dimension. But the eternal is not discovered from within the truncated and fixed imaginations of the damned, which are diminished by infinite repetition of the particular consequences of particular sins. It is discovered by imaginations expanded through repentance and faith. Repentance and faith train the imagination to see properly, rather than simply seeing images as it chooses to see them. The mind learns to see as it relinquishes evil and embraces goodness. As Dante's imagination surrendered and emerged from hell, it began the ascent and saw the stars in a new way. It was ready to climb toward the source of true joy and happiness.

The images in hell are sickening and repulsive. Dante intended them to be so. But in our warped perception of the sins that constitute hell, we also find something attractive about them. Neither attraction nor repulsion alone would do for Dante's poem. Both were needed to capture the nature of hell's agony. This was Dante's genius in the *Inferno*. When he turned to the *Purgatorio*, he still had to show pain, but the pain was mingled with the joy that comes from paradise. In stark contrast to the fixed and ice-cold infinity of hell, Purgatory is a realm of preparation where everything functions to help souls move toward heaven. This includes the arts. When souls orient themselves toward lesser images in the arts, they are better prepared to act in a fitting way toward higher images.[35]

As the poem moves into the *Paradiso*, images light the path. In the radiant presence of God, everything is known in a new way that deepens our ability to see beauty. This is especially true of Beatrice's beauty, which Dante worships in line after line, Canto after Canto. Then, eventually the

---

[35] Charles Williams, *The Figure of Beatrice*, D.S. Brewer, Cambridge (1994), 177.

poem comes to a threshold beyond which Dante's imagination cannot reach, however intensely he wishes to understand:

> In all heaven, the essence most aglow,
> the Seraph that has God in closest view,
> could not explain what you have asked to know.
>
> The truth of this is hidden so far down
> in the abyss of the Eternal Law,
> it is cut off from all created vision.[36]

In canto XXX the perfect height of the perfect image is reached, showing both the possibilities and the limits of imagination, along with a hope that the threshold of our finitude will forever continue to change. The creator withdraws from visibility so that Beatrice is utterly present. She is poised as she marshals images to speak about each state of being, including intellectual light full of love, a living light beyond which he cannot see. In paradise, the voice of Beatrice—the young woman born in Florence in 1266, who once called to Dante's heart in love—has become the sign of a greater, truer love. Dante's entire life and imaginative work were required to grasp the distinction between Beatrice as the beckoning of love and Beatrice as the sign pointing beyond herself toward the One who is love. There was no shortcut. From his first glimpse of the nine-year-old girl on a small street in Florence, Dante's desire to understand love was inseparable from his imagination's growth into the true meaning of the image of Beatrice. She was the bearer of God for him. At the height of imaginative transport, the presence of Beatrice gave way to the presence of Mary, the God-bearer in the fullness of holy flesh. Through the knowledge of God, Mary led him to the final goal—the love of God. He began to forget Beatrice once he encountered the ecstasy of divine love toward the end of the poem, and this is a source of joy for her. Virgil's role was completed at one threshold, as Dante moved toward things that can only be seen in faith. The role of Beatrice was completed at another threshold, when the Virgin Mary allowed Dante to see things that will not fit into written language but that can only be known through grace.

Possibility and hope continue past any work the imagination can do. The presence of the One is felt in Plato's allegory of the cave, Aristotle's account of the love that moves the celestial spheres, and Dante's final vi-

---

[36] Dante Alighieri, *The Divine Comedy*, 91–96.

sion of the luminous image of Mary with her piercing eyes. But the presence remains beyond the reach of any image. The glory shown forth by the sun and the stars must finally serve an unseen creator who is accessible only in another mode, to which imagination and the created universe gladly subjugate themselves. Dante concludes:

> Here my powers rest from their high fantasy,
> but already I could feel my being turned—
> instinct and intellect equally balanced
>
> as in a wheel whose motion nothing jars—
> by the Love that moves the Sun and the other stars.[37]

Everything has its place. As the imagination grows, it sees more clearly how each part of creation plays a part in the act of love that opens the wondering mind to God, other people, and the themes of the universe. Dante's great poem reveals what love is through its images, leading to a great act in which Beatrice is the knowing, and God is the known.

The poem tells a story about how love awakens our souls to the beauty of creation and the creator. But—we must not miss the intensely erotic nature of the love Dante portrays, nor the way this love was enlivened by a very particular girl, on a very particular street, in a very particular town. It might sound strange to say that this is part of why, in striking contrast to Aristotle and Aquinas, Dante gave moral thought a higher place than metaphysical thought. Moral practice fosters the perfection of an individual, including the divine aspect that God provides through nature and grace as an act of distinctly erotic love: love's union with wisdom is the supreme principle of the world. This erotic movement does not occur in metaphysical abstractions of being. It occurs in the particular beings who actually exist. It is bound to action rather than theory, and it is expressed in the concreteness of personal existence rather than in the universal essences that often populate scholasticism. The power of eros draws us higher, and for the sake of the ultimate love, which is love of God, we become humble and we renounce any obstacles to this love.

Philosophy—the erotic union of love and wisdom—shapes us in a way that leads us to love what God loves, which is the fulfillment of what we witness in erotic love between two people. This is why Beatrice is the key to understanding Dante's journey in the *Divine Comedy*. The journey

---

[37] Dante Alighieri, *The Divine Comedy*, 142–46.

most certainly, and concretely, began in the poet's imagination the moment he saw, and desired, one particular girl in front of the chapel doors in Florence. But as he moved toward the poem's final vision of the ineffable and unutterable love of God, he saw the deepest truth of Beatrice: she was loved by God. Because she was utterly loved by God, she was utterly herself, and she could no longer be lost in the way we sometimes are when we try to love in the fog of this world. She was moving toward a vision of perfect participation in the eros of God. Philosophy is always on the way toward this highest love, but on its own it can never bring us to that complete enjoyment. In the *Convivio*, Dante even goes so far as to call philosophy prostitution, though this prostitute is adored.

Dante's poem portrayed the reciprocity of erotic forces coming from God and ascending back to God from the created world. This theological aesthetic, reaching past death and transforming day-to-day encounters with the particulars of the world, is possible only to a philosophical imagination embedded within a created cosmos filled with spiritual powers. Faith-shaped imagination lends a vividness to life by renewing our ability to see radiance in the smallest parts of creation, from the slightest struggling worm to the ecstasy of earthly erotic love. The meaning of everything is converted by the reality of God's creative glory. If philosophy is, in some sense, a beloved prostitute, she is still the servant of God, aiding the incremental transformation of our finite imaginations on the journey. From inside our limits we are called to patience, called to hope. All desire, finally, will find its fulfillment beyond the immediacy of what is desired. But this does not diminish the value of any particular person or thing we desire. Far from it. In the light of a love greater than we can put into words, the particulars are unveiled as part of the glory of creation. But through obedience, they are also prevented from usurping the greater for the sake of the lesser—a usurpation that can only lead to the frozen and repetitive remnants of reality imagined in the *Inferno*.

The final image in the poem is the Celestial Rose, formed of men, women, and the souls of children, with angels like bees bringing God's love to the blessed. Love is God's truest name, and in this love, eros and agape have a nuptial reciprocity. They are finally, for Dante, the same thing. The fullness of this love would not fit into Dante's words, but what he could not say, the archangel made visible, as "the divine eros itself, which by the mediation of the angel glowing with love, rushed down upon the Virgin."[38]

Where Dante embraced the power of images to bring our imaginations to the threshold of divine knowledge, Dionysius the Areopagite rejected the idea that images have analogical power to reveal God's nature. Though every created being has some similarity to its divine exemplar, however faint, and can light our path toward the transcendent, Divine nature ultimately exceeds every thought in mind and therefore must remain unknown. St. Hilary of Poitier likewise described the way the mind falters when it tries to use language to scale the incomprehensible reality of an invisible, ineffable God and finds itself slipping with no secure conceptual hold. We see in a glass darkly. Divine truth appeals to us through faith expressed in images and words, but because these images and words originate in what we perceive through our senses, our knowledge of God always falls short of reality.

Of course, one might also view such imaginative work as nothing more than human deification of the celestial realm. Perhaps imaginations shaped by the false idea of a creator impose so-called "glory" and "radiance" on the universe. But we are still left with a conundrum. Why would humans attribute divinity to the heavens in the first place? Why does humanity seem compelled to deify anything at all? If there is no God, deification of the heavens is merely an imposition of errant imagination. If there is a God, celestial deification arises from something deeper than reason or myth, deeper than logic or mytho-logic. If there is a God, this reality has a structural place in human thought, and the deification of anything is neither purely literal nor purely fictional but rather analogical. We use our intellect to achieve concepts, and these concepts must be chosen, revised, and corrected as we think about the reality of a transcendent God. But we cannot consciously affirm the possibility of transcendent reality unless the possibility seems compelling to us.

Philosophical imagination must be shaped by a habit of the mind to explore the possibility of transcendent reality, just as certain habits of the mind prepare us for investigation in mathematics or poetry. If there is a God, our encounters with this God will not be the same as the passive reception of data. The adventure of seeking the divine is less like a security camera panning the horizon for analyzable information and more like the discovery of a lover. Illumination is the inkling that God is both hidden

---

[38] Hans Urs von Balthasar, *The Glory of the Lord: A Theological Aesthetics, III*, 81.

and revealed in everything we perceive and everything we know. St. Bonaventure described nature as a book written from outside the world: the experience of radiance in the natural world that lights up creation also points us beyond it. Likewise, our thoughts about God, which always fall short, prod us to move beyond our thoughts. Every creature provides a glimpse of its divine exemplar, but its light is always mixed with shadows.

Lovers often quarrel during the uncertainty of mutual discovery, but the quarrels uncover new aspects of mind, heart, and body, especially as the lovers, and the quarrels, mature. Artists and prophets also quarrel. Idols are formed by sculptors who try to express something about God, and iconoclasts destroy these idols, since an infinite God cannot fit into a statue made from one half of a log, while the other half is thrown in the fire to keep the sculptor's workshop warm. Intellectuals create theological and philosophical systems to sum up all that can be said about God, until musicians lay bare the incompleteness of these systems by expressing a mystery through feelings beyond words. Poets write epics populated with the gods, and prophets write revelations they receive from God. Prophets receive their messages from God and stand against the poets who mistake the visions and dreams of their own hearts for truth from above. But prophets still need the poets because prophecy is proclaimed in language, and like Henri de Lubac has pointed out, we must conceive even the objects of revelation.[39]

As the imagination grasps its place and purpose in a created universe, it becomes nimbler in its use of its primary instruments of discovery—metaphor, simile, symbol, harmony, arrangement of form. The roots of imagination, through which it draws its life and light, are planted in the living substance and invisible dynamism of first things, which the imagination expresses through the artifacts of poems, stories, music, paintings, and dance. The poetic apriori is the art of discovering and expressing these ineffable first things, which always appear on the surface of our reality, what we call the world.

Our imaginative responses are evoked by our experiences of what is most real, but our expressions of these experiences are always partial, incomplete, and fallible. Nonetheless, experience must be given the contours of imaginative form if they are going to be shared with others. Imaginative forms objectify our subjective experiences in philosophy, poetry, painting,

---

[39] Henri De Lubac, *The Discovery of God*, trans. Alexander Dru, William B. Eerdmans, Michigan (1996), 97.

music, liturgy, Scripture, and law. Though transcendent reality exists beyond our images and concepts, it nonetheless enters them, and by doing so it becomes the foundation of our knowledge.[40]

Justifying confidence in our knowledge of the world is difficult enough. Justifying confidence in our knowledge of God is much more difficult. We lower the plumb line of philosophical imagination into the depths of God. As it drops, with no hint of reaching bottom, the endlessness itself becomes part of the knowledge. When images seem to get us closer to reality, they have done the beginning, middle, and end of their work. But our minds must move past the image, or else the image will become an idol. Idolatry interrupts the only force that can take us closer to reality, which is love. St. Bernard imagined the mind—continually forming and reforming knowledge—as a swimmer who must move to stay afloat, aware that the movement itself is the support and that to stop is to sink. Imagination is not made of final harbors. It is the energy of mental and spiritual motion that moves from the known into the unknown and back again. We are imaginative creatures who stop imagining at our peril. But if we make our images into fixed idols, we mistake local and transient delights for the true object of desire. It is an ancient temptation.

Dionysius the Areopagite and St. Augustine each found a middle way between the images, which are the servants of God, and the true presence of God as God is. Even when our best knowledge of God carries us further along the path of discovery, it nonetheless might later be denied, or at least revised, once we learn more of the truth. This does not mean our knowledge is not valuable. It only means that it is partial and fallible. When philosophical imagination compels us to move beyond our most cherished ideas about God, we sometimes feel like we are losing God. But if we trust in the central reality of love, we can relinquish our fears. Aquinas drew on Augustine's *De Trinitate* to describe our dynamic and ever-growing awakening to the image of God. Our imaginative journey toward the *imago dei* has three stages. We begin with images of creation residing in all human beings. These enable our creative minds to know and love God. Grace leads us to the next stage in which we develop, however imperfectly, the habits of knowing and loving God. The last stage is beatitude, in which the saints know and love God perfectly through glory: "The

---

[40] De Lubac, *The Discovery of God,* 106.

final solution of the human problem lies in adoration. It can only be found in ecstasy."[41]

---

[41] De Lubac, *The Discovery of God*, 192.

V. Imagination and Mythic Discovery

The Italian philosopher Giambattista Vico was a bit odd, especially for someone living in an age that venerated enlightenment versions of reason. Vico's greatest work was *The New Science*. He seems to have written the book wildly, without parsing distinctions in a way that might satisfy the cool clarity of a mind sequestered from imagination. But he knew what he had accomplished, even if he was the only one in Italy who recognized the importance of his ideas. In a letter to his friend Giacchi, from November 25, 1725, he wrote, "In publishing my work in this city I seem to have launched it upon a desert. I avoid all public places, so as not to meet the persons to whom I have sent it, and if by chance I do meet them, I greet them without stopping; for when this happens, these people give me not the faintest sign that they have received my book, and so confirm my impression of having published it in a wilderness."[42]

Vico was suspicious of the way binary logic categorizes everything as true or not true without remainder. He cared about truth, but he was also captivated by *verisimilia*—things that appear true or that are apparently true. Such things populate the *sensus communis*, which he thought should be formed in the young as soon as possible. His concept of common sense differed from that of Aristotle, Descartes, or Locke. He identified it with the idea of *commune* as a mental property that stands over and above understanding, and which derives from the imagination. Though the sensus communis is not governed by the abstractions of binary logic, it has a deep relationship to logic embedded in a rhetorical context.

Vico's ideas about this relationship were influenced by Peter of Spain. Peter (who was from Portugal, not Spain) appeared in the *Divine Comedy*. He was the only Pope whom Dante placed in paradise. Before becoming Pope John XXI in 1276, he was the physician for Pope Gregory X. His work on logic was influential, but he might have done much more had the ceiling of the Vatican not collapsed and killed him in 1277. Nonetheless, his theory about the translation of enthymemes helped Vico understand how maxims function in the logic of rhetoric.

---

[42] From a letter Vico sent to his friend Giacchi, November 25, 1725. Quoted in Giambattista Vico, *The Autobiography of Giambattista Vico*, trans. Max Harold Fisch and Thomas Goddard Bergin, Cornell University Press, New York (1944), 14.

Enthymemes are incomplete syllogisms with only two terms. An enthymeme is translated into a complete syllogism, which has three terms, by making the middle term explicit. In Aristotelian logic, the middle term of an argument allows us to reason from a major premise and a minor premise to a conclusion. A complete syllogism has this form, with M as the middle term:

Every M is A (major premise)
Every B is M (minor premise)

Every B is A (conclusion)

Peter did not restrict his concept of the middle to the abstraction of the middle term, M. An argument is a reason producing a belief regarding a matter that is doubtful. An argument is abstract, whereas argumentation is an argument that is made more concrete. A question is a proposition that is subject to doubt. A conclusion is a proposition that is confirmed by reasoning. But the middle, in Peter's sense, is the relation between the middle term and the extremes. Relations have context, require insight, and can be more or less fuzzy at the edges. They confirm conclusions, though they do not provide certainty in the absence of context.

An enthymeme lacks a minor premise. Rather than having the structure of a complete syllogism, an enthymeme has this form:

Every M is A (major premise)

Every B is A (conclusion)

In an enthymeme, all three terms (A, B, and M) are present, but B is used only once. Here is a concrete example:

A mortal rational animal runs.

A human runs.

Peter's theory of enthymemes was part of the larger idea of place logic. Maxims take the form of enthymemes. To make a maxim into a proper syllogism, the syllogism must be reconstructed with a minor premise, which means that one must discover the middle term. To find the right argument, one must find the middle term that makes the connection. We convert questions into conclusions by finding the right argument. A place is where one goes to find the right argument.

Place logic allows us to make sense among ourselves. Places are part of the sensus communus, occupying the realms of memory, language, and culture. Our discovery of the grammar and syntax of place logic depends upon what Vico called poetic wisdom. If we do not understand place logic—where to go for arguments that allow us to reason about maxims, or maximum propositions—then we become forgetful and lose access to middle terms. We forget the reasons why our maxims are what they are. We lose our place, which leads to a relapse into barbarism. Vico was not terribly optimistic that humanity can avoid barbarism, but he nonetheless tried to clarify our condition in his big, messy book, *The New Science*. He rooted his project in memory and imagination, because that is where we find the content of the places—the *topoi*.

Topics is the art of connecting concepts and showing links between ideas. It is an art intimately related to the discovery of metaphors, which cannot be broken into their individual elements and analyzed without losing the connections they reveal. Vico develops the principle of the *verum/factum*—the centerpiece of his philosophical method—to shine light on these arts of connection and on the fluid power of the middle term. The principle of the verum/factum is a medium of thought that identifies the true with the made. Donald Verene, the great Vico scholar, described the verum as an intelligibility made by a mind engaged in the process of discovering a middle term.[43] Vico's principle enables us to grasp metaphysical intelligibility in the world, which is to see "the daylight of the divine through the opacity of the bodies of the world."[44]

Vico calls the over-arching rubric of his project poetic wisdom, but this is a wisdom of the whole with a reach that goes far beyond what we usually think of as poetry. It refers to the wisdom arising in various forms of human poesis, the made that Vico identifies with the true in his principle

---

[43] Donald Verene, *Vico's Science of Imagination*, Cornell University Press, New York (1981), 48. In his discussions of Vico's theory of the imagination, Verene has discussed extensively an important distinction Vico makes in *The New Science* between two powers of the imagination, both of which he uses in the development of his phiilosophy, but to different purposes. The first is *fantasia*, which is a primordial faculty through which something is made into an object for human consciousness. The second is *immaginazione*, by means of which something that is already an object for consciousness is formed as an image leading to its conceptualization, its *intendimento* or *concezione*.

[44] Giambattista Vico, *On the Most Ancient Wisdom of the Italians*, trans. L.M. Palmer, Cornell University Press, Ithaca (1988), 77.

of the verum/factum. Poetic wisdom includes history, politics, metaphysics, and even geography and astronomy. He uses a sort of grappling-hook principle of philosophical imagination. When an infinite number of thoughts seem to stand between a first thought and a last thought, we are paralyzed by a Zeno-like paradox. Our minds can only move when we throw our thoughts forward or up through an act of imagination, the way a person climbs a mountain by throwing a grappling hook from ledge to ledge. The imagination uses whatever is within its reach to move past and go higher. Shakespeare hinted at this in *A Midsummer Night's Dream*: "The imagination bodies forth the forms of things unknown."[45]

Philosophical work often begins in metaphor. In a created universe, we can reasonably use a kind of poetic logic to analyze the ontology of metaphor and analogy. Place logic transforms the imaginative reach of philosophy into an adventure in deep realism: when we add to the world under the creative pressure of providence, we discover true things about the *res* (the stuff that is, the things that are), including our created minds and imaginations.

Primal truth belongs to the creator. Only God fully knows creation, because the condition for knowing a thing fully is to make it. We can grasp parts of reality, but we cannot gather these parts into a vision of the whole in the way God can. We make observations and often, we guess. But we never have the creator's direct understanding of the whole. Humanity cannot define the things of creation but only the names of those things. The names humanity assigns to the things of creation arise from the imagination. When we name things that occur in human history, the objects of knowledge are inseparably connected to the subjects who know them. We name such things with an authority that resists dispute, even from God. This includes the history of our efforts to imagine God and to respond to what God reveals through the shaping forces of providence in history, though God is not simply one among the other actors in the story of human history.

Aquinas conceived of the natural world as an order we grasp through contemplation, while the artifacts of human activity constitute an order we create through contemplation. But we have contemplative access to both orders. For Vico, only God can understand the order of the natural world directly, because God alone created it. Our own direct understanding is limited to things that arise from human poesis, the capacity to create that

---

[45] William Shakespeare, *A Midsummer Night's Dream*, V. i. 14–15.

resides in the human mind itself. Even mathematics that applies to the natural world falls entirely on the side of human wisdom. Only God has direct knowledge of creation, but though limited, the human mind can know the moral world manifested in history in a direct way that is qualitatively similar to God's knowledge of creation.

Languages evolve as we name things in the moral world. The history of language is inextricably intertwined with the history of law, custom, war, and peace. This history of the evolution of language is the rich sense Vico gives to the idea of philology. Philology embraces the history of language and literature, along with philosophy and politics. In Vico's sense of the idea, philology is philosophy, since the contours of all that we say about history come from meaningful human thought, disclosing the truth of what it is to be human. But thinking can never be equated with logical precision: when truth first dawns, the human mind initially responds with a kind of abandon and wild enthusiasm, and it is quick to dismiss difficulties and to justify faults as negligible. We would have a difficult problem if we had to choose between a faulty but enlightening excess of love and faith or a closed coldness of indifferent, if precise, analysis. Vico offered a third way we can remain focused on the light without hiding the shadows, a way that Benedetto Croce described as "always endeavoring to play the part of a free but not fanciful interpreter, a warm lover, but not a blind one."[46]

The master key to Vico's work is the idea that primitive humanity was made up of poets who thought in poetic images and whose minds were animated by concrete, vivid, intuitive forces. The human mind first reached toward the world in myths, songs, and verse. Words were living metaphors revealing the structures and interconnections of things, and they were spoken with vibrant urgency, not because of some theory about metaphor, but because this was the manner in which the human mind dwelled among the things of creation. Poetic creation was a necessity for these poets, not an ornament. Their myths were experienced as truth. But eventually the human mind developed the ability to stand back from itself, and the force of the myths tapered as they were transformed into fables and allegories. Under the force of philosophy, the imaginative universals of the poetic imagination gave way to intelligible universals. Socrates was an important figure in this shift, as he introduced irony into human thought and crushed the work of the theological poets, fundamentally changing the

---

[46] Benedetto Croce, *The Philosophy of Giamattista Vico*, trans. R.G. Collingwood, H. Lattimer, London (1913), 42.

ways the mind perceives its relationship to history, myth, and the natural world.

The vibrancy of imagination shrank as the power of abstraction became dominant in the life of the mind. But the primal force of poetic wisdom did not disappear: after lying fallow for centuries, it emerged through the works of a second Homer—Dante. Dante's poetic sublimity broke from the numbness induced by forces that silenced the sensuous aspects of the mind and the wildness of imagination. He marshalled the rough and vigorous images of wrath and merciless punishment in the *Inferno*, the endurance of severely patient moral heroism in the *Purgatorio*, and the intensity of joyful bliss in the *Paradiso*. He stoked the flames of imagination, and he tossed metaphysical abstractions onto the fire of his great poem. His new, primal song was directed to the same God humanity once met on the mountaintop, who spoke in thunder and lightning to the quaking and responsive imaginations of the theological poets.

Vico's most valuable insight is the idea that imagination can be a mode of philosophical thought. Images growing out of the imagination are not merely decorative flourishes for abstract ideas but are the substance of philosophical wisdom and reveal the nature of the minds from which they emerge. In an analogous way, institutions that arise in human history manifest and give substance to humanity's sensus communis, the foundation of all society. These institutions are the places, the topoi, constituting the middle term between the divine and the natural. They arise as providence works in time, and they can only be grasped by metaphysical vision.[47]

Human rationality grew within these institutions made by humans and permeated by providential structures. It did not begin with the reflective intellect that we see in later stages but rather with the more primal powers of memory and imagination, from which imaginative universals arose. Imaginative universals ordered experience for the original minds of humanity. Vico calls this idea of experience ordered by imaginative universals *la chiave maestra*, the master key of his new science. To understand how human intelligibility grew when the human mind's activity dawned, we must understand how imagination created the fables that gave form to human experience, the imaginative universals that first allowed intelligibility. For the original poetic mind, these fables did not function as analogies: reality was constituted by these fables and imaginative univer-

---

[47] Verene, *Vico's Science of Imagination*, 56.

sals, which have "univocal, non-analogical, meanings for various particulars under their poetic genera."[48] Among these particulars, mythic thought discerned identities, rather than mere similarities. Metaphor allowed them to perceive these identities. By metaphor the poetic mind came to know the truth of the world.

We grasp the way that God enters history by understanding and mastering these fundamental metaphors. This is a form of prudence. Generally speaking, prudence is the capacity to see the truth of things. Vico extends the idea: prudence is the ability to read the signs of history and thereby understand the universal law that is the foundation of all societies. Prudence, wisdom, and perception make the intelligibility of the human world possible through the principle of the verum/factum. The physical sciences and the social sciences approach their objects from outside. Vico's science begins within human reality. It is a science of the philosophical imagination and the metaphysical fable. It tells the story of ideal eternal history—*la storia ideale eterna.*

This idea sounded strange to Vico's contemporaries, and it certainly sounds strange to many of us today. But part of the reason it sounds strange to us is that we often approach ideas as though they are objective specimens to be analyzed on the intellectual dissecting table. For Vico, the act of philosophical imagination is something we ourselves must perform to understand. In the *New Science*, he trains our imaginations to carry out this performance as we participate in his work. We begin to experience the necessary metaphysical illumination through our own imaginative exploration of the meaning of the world. If we follow his lead, our imaginative formation allows us to recapitulate the original speech. We gain access to the imaginative universals that make sense of the human world by revealing the invisible—the work of providence in the history of the human mind's creation of language and institutions. This history of imaginative human creation through which first things are revealed is the poetic apriori.

The human mind moves among the languages, institutions, and histories of nations. Vico's *New Science* is a story-telling science that trains us to see the topoi of the human community, the places of the sensus communis. This is why Vico says that "the first science to be learned should be mythology or the interpretation of fables."[49] The mental language we discover in such work begins in imagination, which is itself a form of

---

[48] Giambattista Vico, *The New Science*, trans. Thomas Goddard Bergin and Max Harold Fisch, Cornell University Press, New York (1994), 210.
[49] Vico, *New Science*, 51.

thought. This mental language is the solution to the Tower of Babel. The sensus communis is itself the imaginative act that yields the mental dictionary from which the diversity of articulated languages originates. The connection to the unspeakable first language of imagination, which is the ultimate object of place logic, is reached through the particulars of individual languages. That first language expresses the community of mind, the common wisdom of humanity shaped by an invisible providence, the *vocabolario mentale* that lies below the surface of all particular languages.[50]

If we lose the ability to form the world with our imagination and to see the ways that providence shapes our sense of things through our stories and our institutions, we end up with a kind of barbarism of reflection. We lose touch with humanity's common sense and become subject to the malicious forces of the kinds of people who populate the lowest circles of Dante's *Inferno*—the treacherous people who betray the common trusts that are needed if we are to have civilization. Such people degrade knowledge, language, and institutions. This barbarism endangers all that is valuable to the human community. It renders the imagination powerless by relegating it to the domain of art where it is sequestered from a larger sense of human knowledge. Education breaks apart into silos, and we lose the ability to see the whole that Vico refers to as the *flower of wisdom*. Nations begin to fall when they forget their stories.

Storytelling is not merely a pleasant leisure time diversion. It is the primary way that philosophical imagination grounds itself in memory, which is the root of common humanity. Storytelling is how the philosophical imagination reaches past discrete concepts that are isolated from the truth of the whole. Through the stories it tells, philosophical imagination restores the mind to its proper relationship with both humanity and the divine. This is the deep art of place logic, the power to see the middle term linking the topoi. Even when this power is atrophied, it is still present in our minds. To recover this art, the human imagination must be nourished by memory, the home of what was, what is, and what is to come—the true house of being.

When we form images, we imitate the divine power that makes the invisible visible. The forms we bring into the world are lit up by the same

---

[50] In addition to the term *vocabolario mentale*, Vico uses the terms *dizionario mentale* and *lingua mentale commune*. For a deeper sense of the richness of this *dizionario* see the glossary in Donald Verene, *Vico's New Science: A Philosophical Commentary*, Cornell University Press, New York (2015).

power that lights up the world with beauty. The distinction between the visible and the invisible is philosophically interesting. It prods our imaginations to reach past stunted appraisals of reality that only acknowledge whatever can be measured and to discover how the visible reveals the reality of the invisible and how the invisible reveals the significance of the visible. Certain Platonic strains of thought value the invisible over the visible, as if the surface of a thing exists merely to point beyond itself. But this seems to miss the musical reciprocity between the visible and invisible aspects of reality. Harmony requires both the notes and the silences between the notes. Neither a naturalistic reductionism that eliminates the silences from music nor a misguided Gnosticism that eliminates the notes will ever be adequate to the whole story the philosophical imagination evolved to discover.

The relationship between the imagination and the divine transforms our understanding of imagination's role in the act of compositing the forms of music, painting, dance, and storytelling. The imagination enables active memory not merely to collect past facts about experience but to relate these facts to each other within a meaningful scaffolding. The scaffolding is revealed through the emergent relationship of these facts, as artistic form is revealed through the arrangement of colors, musical notes, or words. The structures of memory and imagination are mutually illuminating, cooperative, and interdependent, and they are revealed through memory's use of images. This art of memory—sister to the art of philosophical imagination—provides maps for the mind that are guides to significance in the natural, magical, and supernatural patterns of human life.

Raymon Lull, Giullo Camillo, and Giordano Bruno were all luminaries in this art. Each of them discovered links between imagination and memory, and each argued for the art of memory as a means of investigating reality. The act of thinking shapes thoughts that are signified by images and held together in memory. Images give form to thought. A camera approaches the things in the visible world, one after another, without registering the significance of connection. But the act of thinking is fundamentally about connecting thoughts that would lose their full significance by themselves. Connection requires the structures of memory. Memory holds the images that give thought its form. Lull, Camillo, and Bruno each made discoveries about this matrix of memory and its relationship to human thought, human imagination, and the primal reality preserved in works of art, myths, and the institutions that emerge from the collective memory of communities.

Raymon Lull was a decade younger than Thomas Aquinas. He was born in 1235, spent his youth as a troubadour, and died in 1316. Francis Yates described the illumination Lull experienced on Mount Randa, an island in Majorca, where he grasped that creation's deepest reality is its infusion with God's attributes.[51] He saw that an art based on these attributes would be universally valid, and he wrote about it in several versions of a book that ultimately found its mature form in his *Ars Magna*. This art of discovery and investigation into reality and truth allowed memory to go beyond its ancient role of merely recollecting facts. It made use of abstractions rather than visual images, like a geometry of the cosmos. In the final version of his work, which eventually became known as the *Ars Ramundi*, he showed how to gather not only what is given in the senses and imagination but also what is beyond either of these in speculation. His art allowed the comprehension of much in little.

There was an interesting quirk in another of Lull's books, *Liber ad memorum confirmandam*, in which he hinted that anyone who wanted to strengthen memory would find the crucial clues to the effort in another essential work of his called *The Book of the Seven Planets*. Unfortunately, Lull never wrote a book by that title. He did, however, write a book called *Tractatus de Astronomia* in which he argued that memory must be based on the *celestial seven*, which became the organizing force of the Theater of Memory created by Giullo Camillo.

Camillo was famous throughout Italy and France for his Theater of Memory. The theater originally existed only in his mind, but with a patron's help he eventually built a wooden version filled with images that, used rightly, allowed a person to see everything hidden in the human mind. Or at least that was Camillo's intention in building the theater. Unfortunately, after Camillo's death in 1544, no trace of the actual theater could be found, and all that remained were stories from his contemporaries, along with a little book called *L'Idea del Theatro* published after his death. The theater rose in seven grades or steps. These were divided by seven gangways representing the seven planets. Like many things in the world of imagination, the theater was topsy-turvy. There were no seats where the audience might be expected to sit. Instead, spectators sat where the stage would normally be, and they looked out toward seven tiers, which represented the seven gates holding the images that constituted the memory

---

[51] Frances A. Yates, *The Art of Memory*, University of Chicago Press, Illinois (1966), 174.

places. In the lower places, Camillo arranged the seven planets—those essential measures upon which all earthly things depend. A spectator's mind was supposed to grasp these first, before moving toward the super-celestial world of the Ideas, which he associated with Angels and the Sephiroth. The mind could also move downward, toward the elemental world. In any case, once the mind grasped the method of the theater, the spectator was supposed to be able to make a speech about the whole.

Written speeches based on the writings of Cicero assisted one in the making of a speech encompassing every subject. The speeches were placed in drawers beneath each of the images. There is a bit of vagueness to the whole thing that is made worse by the fact that the theater was lost after Camillo's death (possibly, some said, taken up whole into the heavens) and by the fact that the big book Camillo intended to write never quite found its way onto paper. We only have his short book, which is not much more than a pamphlet. Francis Yates's description of the theater is very generous to Camillo's sketch of the project. She observes that "when one thinks of all these drawers or coffers in the theater, it begins to look like a highly ornamental filing cabinet."[52] But she also notes that reducing it to a filing cabinet distracts from the grandeur of his idea that memory can be "organically geared to the universe."

Camillo was a Christian Hermetist who tried to combine the classical part of memory with the Hermetic and Cabalist strains that were beginning to flourish in the Renaissance—especially the ideas of Marsilio Ficino, whose work pervaded the memory theater. Both Camillo and Ficino venerated Hermes Trismegistus as a prophet who foretold the coming of the Son of God. Ficino used magical rules to confer the status of talismans upon images. His images were made from astralized myths that shape the imagination. As these images are lodged in memory, a divine power is fostered so that when a person moves about in the world, the external appearances are unified through the inward image, which is itself drawn from the divine world. He believed his poetic and musical incantations, along with his magicized images, could train the imagination to receive celestial influences, changing the way in which we behold the cosmos. This is the poetic apriori.

Camillo borrowed Ficino's solar magic to animate the inward significance of his memory images. Camillo's theater transformed the art of memory through Hermetic magic so that the imagination itself could grasp

---

[52] Yates, *Art of Memory*, 145.

the meaning of the cosmos, not as a mere mortal mired in earthly muck, constructing meaning piecemeal from below but instead as a mind gathering meaning from above: "The mind and memory of man is now 'divine,' having powers of grasping the highest reality through a magically activated imagination."[53] This bordered on heresy in his culture. But Camillo was not condemned, and he supposedly died in Italy with two women in his bed. Unfortunately, not everyone faired so well in sixteenth-century Italy. Giordano Bruno had a much harder time as his mind flamed toward the heavens (literally, alas) in his attempts to show us the wildness of imagination in search of its creator.

The Inquisition reasonably thought of Giordano Bruno as a dangerous man. He wanted to embrace all of reality through imagination and memory. His own memory was stunning in a classical way. When he visited Pope Pius V in Rome, he recited Psalm 86 in Hebrew and then recited it in Hebrew backwards. But his art went far beyond such performances. He associated the development of his memory with divine inspiration. He did not divide the mind into parts but thought the mind as a whole was suffused with the power of the imagination. Like Plotinus he recognized various powers of the mind such as sense, imagination, reason, and intellect, but he thought of them as permeable and fluid, unified by images of variable potency. Imagination's ordering of these images in the human mind reflects the universal presence of divine mind in the world. It is powered emotionally by love, giving it a capacity to reach deeply into the truth of the world as it appears within us and outside of us. The master of memory and imagination draws on both love and magic to grasp the ever-changing forms within the universe, always moving toward unity in imitation of the divine mind. Though Bruno deeply admired Thomas Aquinas, he refused to be restrained by Thomas's rejection of magical arts, and he was daring with his use of magical images in the art of memory.

Bruno's mind and imagination were complex and strange. Like Camillo and Ficino, Bruno leaned toward the magical in his use of star images to achieve a unified vision, aligning inward things to the whole of reality. In *De umbris idearum*, he referred to the magic statues of the *Asclepius*, and he included a list of 150 magic images of the stars. He believed the images of the stars were shadows of ideas, intermediaries between the elemental world and ideas in the super-celestial world. He wanted to see the

---

[53] Yates, *Art of Memory*, 157.

universe with divine eyes, and to grasp the pattern of the world as it appears through a mind shaped and conditioned by the higher celestial spheres of influence that came from the mind of God. Because the lower things are contained in the higher things, we can achieve a truer vision of relationships among the lower things of the world by arranging the celestial images in our memories. Aquinas had given the imagination an important role, but it was limited to corporeal things in the world. Bruno exalted it to a power by which images are used to grasp the intelligible world that resides beyond the appearances. Imaginative investigation of this sort seemed like a form of magic, because magic taps into invisible forces accessible to the mind of one who is open to the idea of a living universe. But Bruno was not merely interested in understanding these forces. He wanted to know how to condition a person's inner world in such a way that these forces could be recapitulated in the mind and made accessible to the thinker. He believed the imagination's conformation to magical forces in the universe could be achieved through his memory systems, and he did not shun the incantations of the sorcerer as he pursued this strange power.

Power to do what? The power to organize the mind from above by gaining access to cosmic forces. Planetary images expressed the powers of planetary deities. If the images were appropriated by memory, the celestial powers would enter the mind, linking the world of the imagination to the stars. Bruno's ideas about this power were influenced by Cornelius Agrippa's *De philosophia occulta* from 1533, but he did not limit himself to Agrippa's astral images. He invented his own images as his imagination discerned the secrets of the cosmic motions that influenced the celestial and sub-celestial world. The power Bruno was pursuing was much more than a challenge to other forms of knowing and ways of organizing one's mind. His images functioned as intermediaries between the super-celestial and sub-celestial worlds. By conforming ourselves to the astral images, we conform ourselves to superior agents. If we understand the images well, they can be manipulated, giving us the power to effect change in lower worlds. Bruno's memory system of magic images, far beyond improving our memory for mere facts and patterns in the universe, is essentially a portal into the deification of a human being. Bruno's memory images grew from his hermetic philosophy, a tradition that believed in humanity's divine origin, connecting us to the celestial powers that govern the world. The images become transformers of the soul, where the archetypal images exist in a confused chaos until the magic images restore order and return divine powers to a person. The Inquisition's displeasure with Bruno's theory of philosophical imagination is not surprising.

Bruno's theory of imagination was specifically philosophical because however much magicians wanted power over the world of things and people, Bruno was most interested in recapitulating the systems of magical images and celestial forces within his own mind, much like mathematics in a physicist's mind. There is beauty in the idea that we can gain access to the order of astral forces by systematizing such images: our vision can be conditioned by the order of the higher worlds, so that we acquire wisdom about the powers governing the machinery of the lower world. There is a thrilling beauty in the idea that there is an order of divine form beyond the celestial world, for which the mind is prepared through mastering the magical images of the memory system. By ordering our minds, we can go beyond the universe itself and reach toward the One whom we desire and in whose shadows we play, work, and think. Order works upon order. The One lends the cosmos a harmony that we reach through imagination, using our discoveries to order ourselves in love and to orient our minds and wills toward the truth of the whole. For Bruno, the truth of the whole, illuminated by the light of the One, was the pearl of great price, and he pursued it with the vigor of a lover.

Bruno's world seems strange. But it is not so much stranger than any other supernatural accounts of the world. The history of all supernatural worldviews begins with a theological interpretation of magic—fairytale worlds in which people sometimes act beyond their own natures, and in which nature itself is made up of beings who can act on their own volition.[54] Stories of magic and fairytales elevate humanity to what exists above it. They draw on our longing to know the mysteries of an invisible creator who can love and be loved. The imagination drapes the veils of its images over invisible ideas that arise from a place beyond the visible machine of the universe. The divine communicates supernatural realities through inspired thoughts that come in the form of images signifying these realities. The images are not themselves the reality, although they indicate the reality. Within the soul an image is marked by a feeling, a glimpse, or a taste of the holy, allowing us to recognize its significance without conflating it with the reality toward which it points. The imagination is both enlivened by and humbled by the distance and disproportion between transcendent reality and the images we are capable of receiving or creating

---

[54] Farrer, *The Glass of Vision*, 13.

through imagination and intellect. Our awareness of this leads to happiness and to acts of worship, because we know the images are only trickles seeping through a dam, behind which is something of incomprehensible magnitude. This is the fundamental work of imaginative philosophy that we call metaphysics.

There is no end to the metaphysical work of the philosophical imagination in a created world, but it is very different from the productive problem solving we usually associate with work. Austin Farrar has argued that there are no metaphysical problems and solutions, only metaphysical mysteries of existence. The philosopher's job is not to solve these mysteries but to describe them, and our descriptions will always fall short. Nonetheless, as we refine our descriptions, our apprehension of the mysteries improves.[55] The philosophical imagination meets the mystery itself in the image, even though the form of the image does not exhaust the reality of the mystery. Different philosophical imaginations give different, and even contradictory, metaphysical accounts of reality that can be read with delight and benefit. They can also be read with hope, because the work of metaphysics is a kind of training that grows the philosophical imagination's capacity to refine, revise, and tentatively accept or reject theories. Along the way, we discover a sense of what is truly illuminating and what is a distraction from the reality toward which an image, metaphor, or analogy is pointing. Our images, metaphors, and analogies always fall short of the reality. Recognizing this is important to the art of the poetic apriori. A metaphysical account might be closer to reality in some ways while farther from it in other ways. And often the work of philosophy brings us to thresholds where the most authentic responses we can make are love, happiness, and worship.

Bruno unfortunately ended his life covered in pitch, diving headlong into the Inquisitors' fire, much to the sadness of the Inquisitors who wanted him to conform to their views and rejoin the fellowship. In a deep sense, Bruno and his Inquisitors were not at philosophical cross-purposes. They both hungered for truth in their own ways. But humility matters in metaphysical dispute.

We can remain humble about our own fallibility, even as we passionately seek a common metaphysical language to express the whole of reality. A truly animated metaphysics is suffused with eros. It is also imbued with a sense of our mortality, because every metaphysical account is the

---

[55] Farrer, *The Glass of Vision*, 63.

work of a dying philosopher, trying to express one last time, in the fullest possible way, whatever wonders have appeared in the course of a short life. Summas create conventions that allow philosophical play to continue or else they provide the foil for rebellion, as revolution is sometimes a condition for revelation. Giordano Bruno, stoked by a fiery imagination, devoted his life to a revolution in the way we view memory. He was in love with a very great mystery, and he wanted to see the truth.

The subject of a great mystery can be loved, even if the appearance of the mystery is analogous to how we appear to our pets: we are present to them in a genuine way that is consistent with the remainder of our reality, but we cannot show them the whole of our reality. This is not because we withhold anything from them and is simply because they are not capable of receiving it. Of course, anyone who has loved a pet knows that an animal can grow into a larger view of who we are. The same is true for our relationship to God. Some forms of divine manifestation may require us to grow to be able to see. And some may go beyond any of our languages, though we will still feel compelled to talk about the experience anyway. We are imaginative, speculative, truth loving, storytelling creatures.

Anyone can see the images in imagination, but faith discerns the meaning of the images. The images are not incidental to a life of faith. They are how meaning becomes accessible to us. The imagination is not a distraction, merely to be endured until we come to rest statically in an imageless heaven of bodiless ideas. Truth emerges through philosophical imagination as we try to grasp the significance of images arising from creation and seen through faith. We cannot give a full account of creation's significance, any more than my dog can give an account of what I am doing right now with pen and paper. But life in this variegated tangle of a universe is the wild adventure of imaginative discovery.

Bruno was a memory artist and a poet whose images, animated by love, approached God's threshold with a divine furor. He knew the limits of abstract thinking, not because such thinking was beyond him but because he was a master of it. He wanted poets and philosophers to become adept at using images that nurture a kind of ontological wonder, to see the significance of forms in the universe where the dull mind sees only shapes. In his own search for truth, he reached deeply into the past for a dark and pagan magic that embraced the One, and for this he was burned in Campo de Fiori on February 17, 1600, before the Theater of Pompey.

As we become more deeply acquainted with the shadows cast in this strange universe, we must also reach toward the light behind them, shaping our imaginations and intellects so that we learn to see "a world in a grain of sand ... Eternity in an hour."[56] As we learn to contemplate the luminous nature of things through imagination and to perceive God as a light shining through our intelligence, we can discover a joyful piety in the act of seeing personality within being itself.

---

[56] William Blake, "Auguries of Innocence," *The Complete Poetry and Prose of William Blake*, ed. David V. Erdman, Doubleday, New York (1988), 490.

VI. Imagination and Created Things

Gerard Manley Hopkins had a hallowed belief: *The world is charged with the* grandeur *of God.* In his work as a priest and a poet he drew on the spiritual exercises of Ignatius and the philosophical illumination of Duns Scotus to find a way to say what his mind and heart felt in a world created and loved by God. He wanted to express the glory of God shining through the radiance of the world. His poems became a form of worship-language brimming with the shimmering light of all that is real. He urgently tried to incarnate what he saw in creation. But because his contemporaries did not immediately understand what he was doing, he also had to develop his own poetics and coin new words to explain what he was trying to capture in his poems. At the center of his poetics was the concept of how the inscape of a thing is instressed within human minds capable of receiving it.

When we experience the inscape of a thing, there is a change in our seeing, though what we register is always already there. To see inscape, the one seeing must be emptied of buzzing distraction and surrender to the seeing as a mode of love, love as agape and love as the fire of eros, a desire that consumes without destroying. Instress is a repetition of experience, in which the order of a thing or situation begins to emerge from randomness, revealing its inscape, which might be too fleeting to catch with one glance. Our minds can approach a thing in an incremental and comprehensively descriptive way and still completely miss its inscape. But we can also approach a thing contemplatively, reaching not for all its discrete parts, instead trying to see its inner unity. This unity is its form, and its form is what makes the *parts* of a thing the parts of a *thing*. In a created universe, everything is a contingent burst of gifted existence. This is the source of radiance that Hopkins does not want us to miss, in even the smallest form of a flower or a worm. That flower or that worm might not have been, and yet it is here. You or I might not have been, and yet here we are. In a created universe, each thing is upheld and made meaningful by its dual character as a thing that is unnecessary and a thing that nonetheless is. In such a universe, there is a power in merely being a particular thing, because the source of all being is the creator. Instress is Hopkins's word for this power within a thing, and inscape is the peculiar form this power takes in any individual thing that is.

Hopkins's radical view of reality grew from his experience of the created world densely populated by inscape throughout. As each form is grasped by a mind that has been made to perceive form, a relationship between the form and the imagination is created. A poet is someone who craves to express this form in language, shaping a poem until the inward flame of the created thing—the flower, the face, the cloud—shines though. Instress implies more than visible radiance. It suggests a kind of force that we experience as urgent, a light not only seen but also felt in a palpable way that must be dealt with. It provokes the passion that leads to poetry or perhaps to liturgy. Poetry is a shared responsiveness to creation's demands and to our own sense of being held in existence with everything else in this collection we call a cosmos.

Realism is sometimes thought of as an orientation toward the world that embraces things as they are, rather than merely as they appear on the surface. But for Hopkins, the contrast between reality and appearance is less an ontological distinction, than it is a distinction in our language between what exists and how we experience existence in sense, thought, and feeling. The appearance of a thing has a kind of being, but a thing's existence is different from its essence (or whatness), and this in turn is different from the source of a thing's being and whatness. For Catholics such as Hopkins, the only exception to this is God, in whom existence and essence are the same. If we are doing epistemology, the distinctions between being, appearance, reality, and essence are probably useful. But the distinctions are merely part of human knowing, because what else would they be? Whether we are talking about the objects of scientific investigation or the significance of imagination's artifacts, once we move from talking about how we know things to talking about the things we know, we have moved from epistemology to the neighboring playground of ontology. Clarity regarding our ontology is crucial for understanding the nature of the philosophical imagination.

Within Catholic theology, the history of thought about essence and existence converges on the analogia entis, the analogy of being. This idea shows us how to move from stories about creation to stories about the ineffable creator. It also discloses the difference between creation and an incomprehensible creator, resisting a conception of God that makes God one more thing among things—albeit a really big and powerful thing—and moves us beyond our mythic stories of Zeus, so thoroughly deflated first by theologians, and later by non-theists. The concept of the analogia entis dissembles our static and comfortable immanent-only mythologies about the divine, and it uses our work in ontology to give us better accounts of God, creation, and that part of creation we call imagination.

Hopkins embraced the idea of the Paremenidean One as a *yes* to being, and the idea of the Heraclitian Flux as a *yes* to the fleeting shimmers that are the forms skirting the surface of being. But neither was adequate to the work of the philosophical imagination that meets things as they are: part of a thing's reality is its glory that draws the contemplative mind out of itself into the grandeur of the world as created by God. This is an awe-filled, or awful, form of seeing, a kind of gazing redeemed by worship. Justus George Lawler, in his eccentric but powerful way, writes that this glance "implies penetration, the sharp edge that gives entrance (and *entrances*) and the power implicit in both notions: penetrate, enter—as when we refer to a glancing blow; that is not merely an oblique blow, but a blow that cuts into, as subject and object cut into each other, interpenetrate and interanimate each other."[57]

In Hopkins's poetry, the feeling of a thing's essence appears as inscape, and the feeling of a thing's being appears as instress. The transformative power of Hopkins's poetry comes from this connection between a theologically framed ontology and a poetics of delight in creation. Instress implies more than visible radiance. It is not merely a light we glimpse. It is a palpable force demanding an urgent response. This force leads us from contemplation to action, to making, to poetry. For Hopkins, everything is charged with God, both in the electrical sense, in which it gives off sparks and ignites fires and in the economic sense, in which all form, essence, and being shimmers through the surfaces of things, awakening creation to its own debt to God for its very being. Creation never comes to an end of this account, understood as the source of further gifts, and as the story of how we come to be who we are.

The metaphor of electricity was a clue Hopkins was only able to glimpse. Our knowledge of the electrochemistry of the brain—that strange object perched among the ideas and images of the world—gives us a deeper way to see through the lens of the metaphor. Who are we to say that the electricity of a created brain is not, in part, a marvelous means for making the music of metaphysics show up in conversation, or on the page, or at the altar? Who are we to say that the poetry of the created cosmos, the verse of the universe, does not fittingly play on the electrical machine of the brain, as thing reaches to thing and points beyond things, that which can only be approached asymptotically with the nimble calculus of analogy? In a created world, we cannot disregard our instrument of reception,

---

[57] Justus George Lawler, *Hopkins Re-constructed*, Continuum, New York (1998), 98.

nor insulate ourselves from the voltage lighting up the physical cathedral of creation, and expect to distill a metaphysics that is true. By metaphysics, I do not mean some esoteric idea that is only relevant at philosophy conferences. I mean the very light in which we see the meaning and goodness of the world. I mean the answer we might try to give if someone asks us why the night sky fills us with longing. I mean the reason we believe our inward compass is reliable, giving our minds and bodies a sense of purposeful direction, so that we can think about what is worth doing in a life and then do it. I think this is a beautiful way to see the world. But it is only the beginning of the story.

We want a metaphysics that is true, like a good compass that registers true North, giving our minds and bodies reliable direction, so that we can think and then move. But true North, alas, is not actually what we see on our compass. The compass points to magnetic north, and the northern magnetic pole moves over time because of the magnetic changes in the Earth's core. The Earth is a big, shifting magnetic, with reversals of magnetic north and south occurring many times over the duration of the planet, a geomagnetic topsy-turvy reorientation that works well as a metaphor for the sometimes-disorienting effects of feeling and other forces on the fragile compass we call our minds. But in the created world of imaginative creatures prone to a stable idolatry, disorientation is sometimes a condition for truer reorientation. The whip the compass needle makes to the left or right because of sadness or ecstasy might indicate that we are near something real and important that we need to understand as the journey continues. Maps have tops and bottoms, but the Earth is round, and the universe is boundless and without a center. If our imaginations are going to reach past its well-trodden path to meet the rest of creation, the behavior of our compass is best taken as a clue to some bonding force that is an adventure, even if it also feels like a threat. We have to trust that God has created us in such a way that our minds are the kinds of things that are meant to encounter creation.

Hopkins suffered from severe depression. We could also say that he suffered from ecstasy. In both cases, he knew the experience of having his mind possessed in ways that threatened his own capacity to keep his wits. So much of what we toil after, and trade our time for, is bound to our attempts to stabilize a world that is teetering on change and dissolution. But we can only see what we can see. When someone cannot see the expansiveness of interplanetary space because their mind is locked in a closet with one flickering light bulb, such a person should be loved with grace rather than judged. If the deep down things are insulated from us by layers of false stories, by our own painful experiences, or by misbegotten tragedies of malformation, the drive to know the truth of things can still drive us toward a dim light. Sometimes, once the door is flung wide, that light turns out to be the sun. And yet, the one we long for disappears over the next hill with laughter, not to escape but to beckon us on to further adventures.

This atmosphere of grace is redemptive. We breathe an air of transformation, not only when we tumble into unexpected radiance but also when we relax into the final meditative silence of the passage we call death. In his poem "God's Grandeur," Hopkins wrote about this radiance:

> The world is charged with the grandeur of God.
>   It will flame out, like shining from shook foil;
>   It gathers to a greatness, like the ooze of oil
> Crushed. Why do men then now not reck his rod?
> Generations have trod, have trod, have trod;
>   And all is seared with trade; bleared, smeared with toil;
>   And wears man's smudge and shares man's smell;
> Is bare now, nor can foot feel, being shod.
>
> And, for all this, nature is never spent;
>   There lives the dearest freshness deep down things;
> And though the last lights off the black West went
>   Oh, morning, at the brown brink eastwards, springs—
> Because the Holy Ghost over the bent
>   World broods with warm breast and with ah! bright wings.[58]

What startles in nature comes from the same source that created both sunrise and sunset. This is not a puzzle to be worked through systematically in the way we find solutions to problems in the laboratory. Instead, it is a fully felt discovery by a prayer-shaped imagination encountering the mystery that resides in the deep parts of reality, demanding not the contained register of a cool and systematic mind but an ecstatic breaking out of homey ignorance into the strangeness of beauty. This disorients us until we see that the landscape is closer to home than anything we have known in the grey mist of the local weather, where we tuck our heads under umbrellas and squint our eyes.

We suspect that we are made for more. We suspect that the ache in our backs and shoulders is not because of overexertion but the result of a

---

[58] Gerard Manley Hopkins, *The Major Works*, ed. Catherine Phillips, Oxford University Press, Oxford (2009), 128. All quotations of Hopkins's poems are from this edition.

constriction of wings that becomes apparent through the presence of a peculiar pain. That pain comes from a disjunction between the way we currently act in the world and the truth of what we are meant to be and to become. The experience—the urge and urgency—of being a creature that is always becoming is a kind of ecstasy. But there is also a pathos in always being on the way, especially when the end toward which we are moving is obscured, leaving us with a vision of our own nature and situation that is partial, incomplete, and sometimes lonely. This is a kind of sadness, where sadness is a placeholder for a feeling that might be called anxiety, dread, depression, ennui, or even madness. The experiences of ecstasy and madness are not mutually exclusive, if only because they often occur in the same soul. The ecstasy of erotic love can lead to the birth of another person, while the wave of madness can lead to someone's death. Though the erotic is enlivening, and though sadness is illuminating, both have been subjected to the cures and consolations of philosophy for millennia. But those who have known passionate love or grief know that more is needed if we are ever to be truly consoled.

We are better off if we remember that philosophy is the love of wisdom, not the possession of wisdom. Philosophy itself is always on the way. Perhaps the best consolation it can offer is to help us understand how partial our wisdom is, so that we can live fully into the strain of this polarity of ecstasy and sadness, where every momentary experience of wholeness and unity is followed by sadness, and every sadness is embedded in a world full of small shimmering ecstasies. Philosophy is the conversation we have on the journey. It is the eruption of observation and commentary among pilgrims who travel to strange, wonderful, and dangerous lands, not people who set up shop in a harbor. Such conversations may never lead to final answers or systematic completeness, but they can lead to better questions by making us better questioners.

The Garden of Eden is the beautiful and frightening myth of our ongoing journey. When Adam was alone in the garden, there was a kind of unity in creation. The elements of the natural world were what they were, and they did not bend back on themselves to behold their own incompleteness and contingency. There was a unity, but there was also a nascent sadness in Adam's consciousness. Adam could not recognize it but God did. It was not good that Adam was alone. So the animals were formed, and God waited to see what Adam would name them. Whatever name Adam gave to them, that was their name. The friendship of Adam with the animals was a part of creation celebrated by the saints. But it was still not enough companionship. So God formed a different companion, another person for whom Adam began to long. He became more of who he truly was by realizing that in some way he was not complete in himself. Only with her did he taste completeness. But even that taste of completeness was not the final destiny. That taste was a goad toward something that was as ineffable to Adam and Eve as it is to us.

In the myth two things came into the cosmos that did not exist before: there was the glimmer of what we long for, and there was the opportunity to mistake the glimmer for the thing itself. Waking up to one's contingency and incompleteness is necessary for the journey. But this awakening makes it possible to mistake the harbor for the journey, the gift of respite in the inn for arrival at the destination. Such is the dawn of the knowledge of good and evil: we can be true to our nature, or we can repeatedly interrupt the forward energy of eros that is meant to drive us further in and further up on our ecstatic journey and instead become caught in a cycle of erroneous and momentary satisfaction. It takes a very great force to make us step out of that impotent repetition and continue on the journey. That force is the looming specter of death. Our only way forward is to be banned from the garden so that we cannot reach the tree of life and become susceptible to a truly interminable cycle of repeated momentary ecstasies, followed by sadness that drives us back into craving for ecstasy. Our salvation lies ahead, and death is the hound that keeps the caravan moving forward.

John Henry Newman received Hopkins into the Roman Catholic Church in 1866. Newman thought of poetry as a kind of speech in which our deepest heart speaks to the deepest heart of another. Hopkins was concerned that poetry was self-indulgent and too individualistic. He changed his mind when he read Duns Scotus, whose work deeply affirmed Hopkins's poetic idea of inscape. Scotus argued that we have direct knowledge only through the this-ness (*haecceitas*) of particular objects in this world. He rejoiced in the particulars of this world, including the particularity of his own heart. For Hopkins, this lit up both the created world and the inner world of mind and imagination. In his notes on spiritual exercises, he wrote that human nature is highly pitched and distinctive and must have evolved from the stuff of world, not by virtue of lower forces but under the influence of a force higher and more finely-pitched than itself. This is especially true for the activity of the mind, which is capable of self-consciousness, including the unique feeling and taste of our individual selves: "Searching nature, I taste *self* but at one tankard, that of my own being. The development, refinement, condensation of nothing shows any sign of being able to match this to give me another taste of it, a taste even resembling ..."[59]

Hopkins describes a singular insularity, but one which longs to be seen and to be spoken. Interior experience is different from exterior expression. Our ability to express ourselves is a gift, but it is a gift that changes us and constitutes a kind of sacrifice. This is part of the complexity of human sexuality, which is deeply related to the urgency of our search for meaning in creation. Virginity—not merely in the physical sense but in the sense that Mary Magdalene was venerated as a *virgo intaita* because of her single-minded passion for Jesus—is the state of oneness. The interior and the exterior are fused. But there is a play in virginal intactness that deepens the sense of what is given in the gift, and what is received, and of how the growth of a person is fostered when the gift is given: a person can become more virginal by relinquishing one form of virginity and uniting with another person. This is the erotic fulfillment of the spiritual injunction that one must lose oneself to find oneself, an imitation of the act of God that Hopkins described a couple of years later in his notes on the spiritual exercises: "God's utterance of himself in himself is God the Word, outside himself is this world ... The world, man, should after its own manner give God being in return for the being he is given or should give him back the being he has given by great sacrifice. To contribute then to that sacrifice is the end for which man was made."[60]

What can we sacrifice? Our time? Our limbs? Our life? Our self? Yes, all of these. But in the strange economy of grace in which we find ourselves by losing ourselves, putting off these things is putting off the things that confine us. The terror and attraction of death is that it might be dissolution or it might be a transcending of limits. Which is it? The question shines light on the ways Western poets have tenaciously linked authentic sexual connection between two people with the act of dying. Both forms of letting go leave us with the taste of our instability and conscious unease. If our urgent questions lead us to practice an honest ontological phenomenology, we eventually realize that the unstable fault line runs through the middle of our own souls and bodies. We try to keep the world whole by creating our stories, poems, myths, and philosophical treatises. But mere making never satisfies us, because even our connections deepen

---

[59] Hopkins, *The Major Works*, 281–82.
[60] Hopkins, *The Major Works*, 282.

our awareness of the duality of our existence. Nonetheless, we are compelled to express the unity we glimpse through our aesthetic, sexual, and mystical experiences, because these reveal to us, however faintly, something besides the darkness of the abyss we peer into as we stand on the threshold of death. The experiences rescue us, in a literally momentary way, from the stretch of time reaching into the untouchable past and future. They remind us that the only part of time that we can call home is now, so we should fully do what we are doing and fully see what we are seeing. Such is the ecstasy Hopkins reaches for as nature is lit up by the supernatural in "The May Magnificat":

> When drop-of-blood-and-foam-dapple
> Bloom lights the orchard apple
>   And thicket and thorp are merry
>   With silver-surfed cherry
> And azuring-over greyball makes
> Wood banks and brakes wash wet like lakes
>   And magic cuckoocall
>   Caps, clears, and clinches all—
>
> This ecstasy all through mothering earth
> Tells Mary her mirth till Christ's birth
>   To remember and exultation
>   In God who was her salvation.[61]

Hopkins the priest was drawn toward the mirth of the Mother of Christ, in whom nature became more fully itself by being carried beyond itself. He distilled feeling from nature, and connected cosmos and creation in his leap from the magic of a calling cuckoo and the ecstasy of mothering Earth to Mary remembering her God. Such an act of imagination shows a kind of philosophical charity and play that does not merely console but that gives us courage to hurl ourselves into the world, trusting in spiritual laws that we have only begun to meet as in a dream. We are creators inside creation finding home. Hopkins bodied forth in his poetry the joyful humility of the analogia entis that mediates between the infinite separation of creator and creature that we see in Karl Barth, and the partnership of creator and creature we see in Alfred North Whitehead's vision of constructing the world. He wrote "God's Grandeur" to show us the ecstatic wildness of nature that is never spent and that is filled with a dear freshness that lives deep down things as the Spirit broods over them with warm

---

[61] Hopkins, *The Major Works*, 140.

breast and bright wings. He wrote "Pied Beauty" to show us the Earth full of dappled things, where the peace we pray for in our liturgy must be a peace among discordant elements, a peace of contrasts.

Because the unity of God is singular and not susceptible to imitation, the inscape of anything that is created is beautiful in itself—it will be dappled, it will be couple-coloured. If we want to experience things as gifts, we must learn to see in a way that does not impose a false unity by dissolving things into the manageable abstractions of generalized laws and concepts. The impulse to abstraction is understandable, with a laudable and revealing aim, and it can be motivated by an impulse toward worship. But beauty, truth, and goodness show up concretely in the world. The inscape and instress of radiant things reveal a creator who sustains creation through an unfathomably intimate presence, while being utterly and unfathomably different from creation. This is the beautiful but difficult concept of God's relationship to creation expressed in the idea of the analogia entis.

Duns Scotus taught Hopkins the philosophical expression of the unique way things body forth in the experience of inscape. He gave Hopkins a philosophical frame for the fundamental language of nature that Bonaventure witnessed in his own worship, inspired by the beauty of the stars. Rather than seeking for a false unity in abstraction, Hopkins's poetic imagination was schooled in ways of reading the contrasting forms of nature. Nature is a language that speaks the unspeakable through its radiant forms. Hopkins answered this with a language of his own in his poems, as he journeyed toward the mystery of God—a creator who does not merely dwell beyond the things but who lights up creation from inside.

Hopkins experienced no clear line between a natural and a supernatural perception of the creator and creation. In both cases, the love of God is the only answer to disorientation. He showed us how the converted imagination can relearn to see the source and sustainer of all created things through the things themselves, lit by an internal light. This is true for the highest celestial object, but it is also true for the face of the next person we see on the street. In a journal entry from 1871, he wrote, "What you look hard at seems to look hard at you, hence the true and false instress of nature … Unless you refresh the mind from time to time you cannot always remember or believe how deep the inscape in things is."[62] He tried to hold true opposites together as an expression of creation in its endlessly varied

---

[62] Hopkins, *The Major Works*, 204.

difference from God, whose divine language of love is spoken through the prismed light of creation. The symphony of contrasts in a poem like "Pied Beauty" is a form of rejoicing in the beautiful mess to which the converted imagination bears witness.

The idea of the poetic apriori resonates with Hopkins's conviction that words bring to mind the Word, the source of all words. The first line of "Pied Beauty" is a poetic statement of the analogia entis, turning toward the things of creation in joy and awe because they are from God and therefore must be connected to God. That connection is the only true link between the universal and the particular, the abstraction and the concrete. The converted imagination in a world of created things sees the unifying source of the multiplicity through the internally illuminated things themselves.

Joy and despair were among the opposites Hopkins held together in his vision of God's good creation. In the "Sonnets of Desolation" he gave an account of the tormented mind, witnessed from within his own struggle with depression. A mind susceptible to such dulling and sadness needs something other than itself to arrive at a place where it can see the truth of things. Hopkins believed—or at least hoped—that the contemplation of beauty can heal the mind and cure the soul when it is coupled with the practices of caring of others and sacrament. If the world's truth, beauty, and goodness register in an individual only as they are embedded in the whole, perhaps there is also a collective aspect to mind in the universe that can give the gift of healing to a singular mind. When we are given a gift, the gift becomes our own. We borrow wholeness, but once we are whole, it is truly ourselves who are whole: if our deafness is healed, we hear with our own ears, if our blindness is healed, we see with our own eyes.

Poetry can disclose inscape. When we awaken to the inscape of a thing, we see the thing more perfectly. This contemplative act brings us closer to the true, the beautiful, and the good. Thomas saw that in so far as the thing is, it is good. He saw the equation between the true, the beautiful, and the good. The more we learn to acquiesce to reality revealed in creation, the better we learn to see this equation. Such insights change how we live in this world, because we learn to see beauty everywhere as we learn to see what is. For those who live in a created world, and know they do, every act of seeing what is real becomes an act of learning to see beauty, goodness, and truth. As we learn to see, we want to tell others about the experience. Ontological wonder makes us pick up our pen, paintbrush, or musical instrument to say what we see. When we do this well, we learn to see much more. This is seeing the world in a grain of sand, seeing eternity in an hour. Even a jail cell made of stones is made of stones that are themselves beautiful.

In a created world, to begin with a particular thing is not to end with a particular thing. Our imaginations are pliable, and we can always reach farther. We reach the instress of things by perceiving a thing's inscape, which is baptized form, a gift of form that is full of meaning because the gift has a giver. The leap from the particular to the absolute is a leap from gift to giver. But we do not leave the gift behind. In a Platonic universe, we gladly exchange the shadow world for the world of forms. But a created thing that is a shadow of its creator becomes more fully itself the more it is seen in its true relationship to the whole. In creation, things are known in an epistemological trajectory that arcs toward relational happiness, rather than mere knowledge of catalogued facts about the world. This arc does not lead toward the encyclopedia but toward ecstasy. The deepest mystery in our adventure of knowing is the felt relation of all contingent, particular things to the One who is their source, sustenance, and reason for being, the One who shows up in stories as the just judge, the ecstatic lover, and the sometimes-outrageous comedian. We weep, desire, and laugh as we tell our stories on the road, knowing that both the road and the journeyers—ourselves—are created by the One toward whom the road is leading. We brood, grow sad, fall in love, and devise pranks. These modest tools are what we use to plumb the depths of the incomprehensible we meet in the poetic apriori.

Poets like Hopkins experience the created world as lit up and suffused with meaning, and they have important things to say about the philosophical imagination. But there is another way to explore the role of the imagination in human life: we can listen to a philosophically inspired poet who was filled with wonder at the idea of the divine but who did not believe in God. In the work of such a poet, only the mechanism is exposed, because there is nothing else to expose: there is no inspiration beyond the fictions we create in an otherwise lonely universe. Wallace Stevens wrote, "Things that have their origin in the imagination or in the emotions (poems) very often have meanings that differ in nature from the meanings of things that have their origin in reason. They have imaginative or emotional meanings, not rational meanings."[63] Stevens made many discoveries about

---

[63] Wallace Stevens, *Collected Poetry and Prose*, ed. Frank Kermode and Joan Richardson, Library of America, New York (1997), 825.

imagination, reason, and the mind as he paid attention to his own experience of an accidental, purposeless, uncreated universe in which the reality of the divine is bracketed, and the only minds that show up are our own meaning-making minds full of longing and compelled to tell stories about the world.

VII. Imagination and the Lonely Mind

Wallace Stevens was a beguiling poet, deeply aware of the difference between living in a created world and living in an uncreated world. He was also aware of the complex experience of believing that he lived in an uncreated world, while retaining the memory and habits of a person who experiences the universe as meaningful. In his poem "Esthetique du Mal" he wrote, "How cold the vacancy / When the phantoms are gone and the shaken realist / First sees reality. The mortal no / Has its emptiness and tragic expirations."[64] His response to being shaken by this reality, in which the phantoms are gone and the vacancy is cold, was to make poetry. But he believed the imagination can discover a new beginning after it awakens to reality, and it can still say yes to the world, even though that yes inevitably tapers into a doomed, dead void. Stevens wrote hymns for the unbeliever. His hymns are full of surprise and delight. The mood for this poetic world suffuses the poem "A High-Toned Old Christian Woman," where he gives an early nod to one of his guiding themes—the idea of a supreme fiction: "Poetry is the supreme fiction, madame / ... In the planetary scene / your disaffected flagellants, well-stuffed, / Smacking their muzzy bellies in parade ... / May, merely may, madame, whip from themselves / A jovial hullabaloo among the spheres. / This will make widows wince. But fictive things / Wink as they will. Wink most when widows wince."[65]

 Stevens's ear was tuned to the music Dante evoked in the *Paradiso*—the harmonies of the one and the many that winged their way beyond his powers to say what his soul had seen. The same music echoes in other poets who resonate with his own jovial yes, whether it is Hopkins with his residuary worm or Arnold scribbling out some circumambient gloom, poets who listened for the mind beneath the world as it appears. But there is an important difference between listening for a divine mind that might be there and listening for such a mind in a universe vacated by all benevolent ghosts. A poet who feels compelled to listen while believing there are no minds but ours can feel terribly vulnerable being situated tenuously inside the coil of a fragile and temporary mortal body, upon which its own poetic existence depends. Perhaps it is fitting that Stevens—aware

---

[64] Wallace Stevens, „Esthétique du Mal," *Collected Poetry and Prose*, ed. Frank Kermode and Joan Richardson, Library of America, New York (1997), 282–83. All quotations from Stevens's poems are from this edition.

[65] Stevens, „A High-Toned Old Christian Woman,"47.

of the darkness but creating jigs and nursery rhymes for adults inhabiting a fictional world—sold insurance to protect against the whims and taunts of chance. For people who want to go on indefinitely like wax flowers on a mantelpiece, insurance is one way to shore up the illusion that this is possible.

The object of poetry is reality itself, which is always full of change and flux, even when it seems as motionless as a stone. When the imagination manifests itself through the words of a poem, it creates movement among apparently static things. A complete account of reality includes the reality of unreal things, like the images Plato used to construct his philosophical view of the cosmos, which Coleridge called "dear gorgeous nonsense." But when we no longer feel the force of fables and myths, the world we experience is emptied of ghosts, gods, and souls whether or not they actually exist. We are only left with the poem itself. A poem is all imagination, and a realist must accept its peculiar reality for what it is. We can understand the poem and its imaginative form of reality without believing in divinities or abstract entities. But the poem does have a kind of reality—it really is. There must be degrees of reality. The imagination can relate to reality in its various degrees, but this relationship can falter under the force and pressure of reality itself—the forces of external events or the forces of mental events beyond our powers of contemplative serenity. Sometimes events such as wars exert forces so potent that they change our ability to imagine, ending one form of imagination and inaugurating a new one. The same might be said for some mental illnesses—schizophrenia or severe depression, for example—in which our perception of reality changes.

We cannot return to the reality lived by Dante. His enormous imagination was tethered to hell, purgatory, and paradise and was populated with the dead who lived on in a different form. Our imaginations are different from Dante's imagination because our reality is different from his reality. Dante's imaginative use of the things in the world depended upon the stories that shaped his reality. Because our minds are abstracted from these stories, we are left with nothing but the things in the world and our transient presence among them. This changes the kind of poetry we write, because poems emerge from our lived experience among the things of the world. When our possible lives change, so does our possible poetry. For Stevens, reality as a whole comprises things as they are, our imaginative presence, and the imaginative presence of others who make up what we call society. The idea of the whole is an interdependent relationship of things as they are, plus imagination. This whole is the content and subject of poetry. The purpose of the poet is to share imagination, lighting up the minds of others so they can live among things and other people in a more interesting way.

The world is made from the senses and the imagination. This gives power to the poet: poets create the world by creating the supreme fictions through which we conceive the world. Imagination conforms to the reality it makes, and reality equally conforms to imagination. Imagination pushes back on reality to survive, and by doing so it changes our perception of things. We make the world in which we live the way a bird makes a nest. Poets and philosophers make worlds, and as poets and philosophers come and go, worlds come and go. But we are nonetheless compelled to make a world with reason and imagination during the short time we are here.

When poets are not making worlds, much of their work involves portraying their own minds, where imagination lives. Of course, the mind of the poet is one of the things in the world, and it interacts with other things in the world. When it brings about ways of seeing things in the world, it does so purposefully, with what Henri Bergson called "forward movement."[66] The progress to which Bergson refers is that of saints and mystics. Stevens's own conception of the supreme poetic idea is very close to Bergson's: it is the idea of God. This might seem surprising, since Stevens was not a theist. But this supreme poetic idea best captures Stevens's sense of the poet's aspiration and inspiration: "If we are able to see the poet who achieved God and placed him in his seat in heaven in all his glory, the poet himself, still in the ecstasy of the poem that completely accomplish his purpose, would have seemed ... a man who needed what he had created, uttering the hymns of joy that followed his creation."[67] Poetry has the power to make the incredible credible. It must do this because poetry is conceived with reality, and reality must finally be credible. The poet wants to say true things, even if the truth the poet says is a truth the poet needs. But the poet's needs are also part of reality. Need is a clue to reality, though its meaning is an open question that cannot be answered by the character of the mere need on its own. In any case, when the poet writes a poem that accomplishes what feels like agreement with reality, he or she believes the victorious poem to be true, at least for a while. This is a source of pleasure and delight.

---

[66] Henri Bergson, *Two Sources of Morality and Religion*, trans. Ashley Audra and Cloudesley Brereton, University of Notre Dame, Indiana (1977), 58.
[67] Stevens, *Collected Poetry and Prose*, 674.

Metaphysicians make ontological theories about reality. Poets do not. Poets bask in the radiance of reality as it shows up in one thing after another, in no particular order. Things register within the poet, flavored by personality, history, and everything else that makes up a person. The truth of a poem is measured against this total experience—the thing and the poet encountering the thing. A thing can provoke the poet's imagination, and the poet's imagination can illuminate the thing. The poem never offers perception apart from the person of the poet: what would that even mean? But it does shine its peculiar light on the thing, and it reveals something true about the thing, or at least about the relation between the thing and the imagination. Stevens's vision of this reciprocity between a poet and a thing resonates with Hopkins's account of instress and inscape, though the machinery operating in Hopkins's universe is very different. In both cases, the poets share their imaginative acts so that we can see the world in a peculiar light. They awaken our faculties and help us see things in a new way. But even though poets bring about this change within us, we still see the world through our own thoughts and feelings.

Things resemble other things. We identify a dog because it resembles other dogs. Resemblance holds the world together. The deepest form of resemblance—the analogia entis—can only occur in a created cosmos, because an uncreated cosmos can only have the purpose and meaning ascribed to it by minds like ours. Poetry plays on resemblances. If there is no meaning or purpose to be discovered in an uncreated universe, taken as a whole, how does resemblance work in the poetic imagination? How does an uncreated world hold together?

In nature we can see the resemblance of one tree to another tree, and this perception of resemblance works well when we are comparing things like oak trees to things like pine trees. Resemblance tapers at the edges when we move from the world of trees to the world of bushes, then grasses, then algae. Metaphor is at the heart of poetic metamorphosis. It can express three forms of resemblance, all of which depend on the activity of the imagination. Metaphors express resemblances among parts of reality, resemblances between real things and imagined things, and resemblances between two things that are imagined (as when we say that God is good, asserting a resemblance between two concepts Stevens believes are imaginary—the concept of God and the concept of goodness). All resemblance is an act of imagination. Because resemblances bind things into the world as we experience it, the structure of reality is "adult make-believe."[68]

A poet's imagination uses reality. But a poet does not own his or her imagination. Imagination is always larger than the poet, borrowing not only from nature but also from collectively built forms of civilization, what Vico called the sensus communis. Imagination is mystical in its reach for ways to express our sense of the beautiful, the erotic, the uncanny. This mysticism can orient itself toward things that occur in nature or toward things we build together, institutions created as imagination meets and uses reality. Imagination is integral to everything the mind receives and gives. Eventually, the cosmos no longer feels made up of images and imagined resemblances but feels simply real. This real world—the final world on which we close our eyes at the moment of our death, when all the work of world-building is finished—is the only reality we can have. Poetry's only tether to reality is the poet's mind. For Stevens, this view of the world-making poetic mind is analogous to the ordering, transcendent reality in which Dante and Bruno believed.

"Is there an imagination that sits enthroned / As grim as it is benevolent, the just / And the unjust, which in the midst of summer stops / To imagine winter?"[69] Here, Stevens asks a good question. The imagination eludes and crosses moral categories, as it eludes and crosses seasons, dipping into winter while the body sweats in summer heat, accompanying the world but directing from the throne, a play throne that in one sense does nothing and in another sense organizes everything, like Stevens's jar in Tennessee. Imagination is the power of the mind over a wilderness of possibilities, including the possibilities of the meaning and value attaching to things and thoughts as they appear before the throne. Imagination shines its light upon things. If it does so in one way the yield is metaphysics, if in another the yield is art. Stevens sees nothing romantic in this liberty of mind: "The romantic is a failure to use that liberty. It is to the imagination what sentimentality is to feeling."[70] Imagination is an ordering power, a domain in which reality registers with all its forms, feelings, and conflicting values. It nurtures our way of seeing by bringing an unreal order into chaos so that we see more than chaos, imposing a value but never satisfied until it hits upon the supreme poetic idea: "If the imagination is the faculty by which we import the unreal into what is real, its value is the value of

---

[68] Stevens, *Collected Poetry and Prose,* 688.
[69] Stevens, „The Auroras of Autumn," 360.
[70] Stevens, *Collected Poetry and Prose,* 728.

the way of thinking by which we project the idea of God into the idea of man."[71]

The belief that the world is uncreated can be disorienting to an imagination that needs God as its greatest poetic idea. The imagination is second only to faith for organizing the cosmos and creating our place in it. Imaginatively shifting from the created to the uncreated is different than shifting from the created to nothingness. The imagination allows a diminishing faith to frame the world as merely uncreated, rather than framing it as nothingness. When we come to see the world as uncreated, we turn from belief in divine revelation to a focused awareness of our own power. Our power in an uncreated world is astonishing, because there is no truth apart from our truth, and our only allegiance is to the logic of that truth.[72]

We can be loyal to the truth of the world, as long as we understand it as the poetry of the world, arising from imaginative minds that emerged in a purposeless, accidental universe like stars, rocks, and trees. The poet reaches for what is harmonious and orderly, reaches for what Plato called the Good. Stevens believes this is almost exactly what the poet reaches for—the Good but the Good as a kind of substitute for a God who, if God existed, would transform mystical poetry into prayer. Poetry as prayer was not a possibility for Stevens. But he was compelled by poetry's power to reach for the Good, to delight in harmony and order, and to find inside a poem something so wonderful that he wonders whether or not we even need to ask about the meaning of a poem. The answer for Stevens is surely no, since he accepts no meaning beyond the meaning we make—human poesis. If God existed, the answer might be yes: if there was a real mystery underlying, pervading, and motivating the very poetry that Stevens finds so redeeming to the human mind, we would want to know.

Skepticism about the possibility of God in this complex world does not diminish our need to grapple with the unknown. Our partial perspectives, our experience of evil in the world, and the tenacious irrationality of our own thinking keep us on the threshold of the unknown. The possibility of insight into this vast unknown is deeply seductive. We are drawn past the ephemeral and transiently shimmering completeness of what we take as the known. When we pay even modest attention to the frayed hems of our best knowledge, we awaken to both the terror and the hilarity of our tumble toward what lies beyond, hymned in poetry's ongoing expansion

---

[71] Stevens, *Collected Poetry and Prose,* 735.
[72] Stevens, *Collected Poetry and Prose,* 750–51.

and repair of the tapestry of our frail worldviews: "Time is a horse that runs in the heart, a horse / Without a rider on a road at night. / The mind sits listening and hears it pass ... // Felicity, ah! Time is the hooded enemy, / The inimical music, the enchantered space / In which the enchanted preludes have their place."[73]

Poetry is an act of imagination that has the power to organize a world. Though Stevens thought the modern imagination had moved away from belief in God, he also thought the idea of God is, and always has been, the world's central poetic idea and the mind's most potent organizing force.[74] He did not believe in God, but he did have an almost Anselmian imagination that hurled itself toward the kinds of limits that culminate in that than which nothing greater can be thought. Our experience of the meaning of life's tragedies and comedies depends upon whether we see these limits without believing that God exists or if we see them and, like Anselm, conclude not only that God exists but that God must exist. This fundamental difference shapes our sense of the world, from which our poetry arises. If God is the major poetic idea in the world, what we do with the idea of God guides our poetry, our theory of imagination, and our perception of the imaginative order of the world. If the central poetic idea is the idea of God, but God does not exist, our imaginations must find a new sense of what it is to be at home in the world. This can be terribly disorienting at first, like being cheated on by a lover you trusted. Stevens calls this feeling panic in the face of the moon: "Panic because / The moon is no longer there nor anything / And nothing is left but cosmic ugliness / Or a lustred nothingness. Effendi, he / That has lost the folly of the moon becomes / The prince of the proverbs of pure poverty."[75]

When the gods dissolve into nothing, we are left with an enormous sense of loss, even though we are still alive and awake in the world, with imaginations that are as active as ever. The gods cannot be replaced by imaginative will: we actually believed in the gods, and we cannot generate meaningful faith in something we simply make up, any more than we can worship a log carved into an idol once a prophet has shown us the folly of cutting down a tree, and worshiping half while using the other half to fuel the fire on which we cook our dinner. If the gods truly arose from our naive imaginations, once we see their true origin, we will never again submit to them, unless we crave comfort more than reality—a false insurance policy.

---

[73] Stevens, „The Pure Good of Theory," 289.
[74] Stevens, *Collected Poetry and Prose,* 806.
[75] Stevens, „Esthétique du Mal," 282–83.

After such a loss, we still catch glimpses that make us doubt our doubt. We feel the long shadow of God retreat, but a shadow is always a shadow of something. We may not have heard an interpretation of this shadow that compels us to capitulate to faith—so many accounts sound suspiciously like variations on ourselves—but we still have an unsettling sense that there is more to the story. Perhaps there is no God. But perhaps the true work of skepticism is to free our imaginations from small gods, so that we can find something deeper behind our poetic and philosophical ideas, which in turn enlivens our imaginations. This possibility hovers over both our poetry and our philosophy as we reach for we-know-not-what. Stevens was moved by Bruno's discussion of Copernicus, who found his way from the cramped prison of his own timid assumptions to the idea of a vast and beautiful universe inhabited by infinite creatures and endless new worlds, each of which mirrors the splendor of their divine creator.

There is a kind of philosophical thought that excels in sorting through the things of this world, especially those we explore in science. In an uncreated world, the imagination can carry us beyond the philosophical inventory of the local world into the poetry of the local world in surprising and beautiful ways. But because the imagination is governed by the limitless limit of the poetic idea of God, there is always a lingering what if? In a journal entry from August 10, 1902, Stevens recorded his own haunting doubt, which he experienced in the transept of St. Patrick's Cathedral. He thought of our response to nature as the world's true religious force. But standing in St. Patrick's, the conflict between the religious forces of the church and nature suddenly disappeared. He saw neither of them very clearly, but he felt himself drawn like a priest to the one and a poet to the other: "As I sat dreaming with the Congregation I felt how the glittering altar worked on my senses stimulating and consoling them; and as I went tramping through the fields and woods I beheld every leaf and blade of grass reviewing or rather betokening the Invisible."[76]

What if we change one thing about reality? What if we join Anselm and imagine God not merely as Stevens's central poetic idea but as actually existing? Call it a thought experiment if that helps. If God does exist, does that change the effect of Stephens's poetry and his ideas about the imagination? The question can be tested on lines like these: "A woman walking in the autumn leaves, / Thinking of heaven and earth and of herself / And looking at the place in which she walked, / As a place in which each thing

---

[76] Stevens, *Collected Poetry and Prose*, 929.

was motionless / Except the thing she felt but did not know"[77] or, "After the final no there comes a yes / And on that yes the future world depends. / No was the night. Yes is this present sun ... / It can never be satisfied, the mind, never"[78] or, "We say God and the imagination are one ... / How high that highest candle lights the dark. / Out of this same light, out of the central mind, / We make a dwelling in the evening air, / In which being there together is enough."[79]

Because of Stevens's fascination with the idea of God, I like to read his poems from inside what I imagine his world to be and then reread them from inside the possibilities available to the imagination if an incomprehensible God created the universe. His poems evoke the feeling of philosophical ideas, ideas such as the ontological difference between something that can feel the whatness of things and something that cannot. His poetry ushers the imagination into such a peculiar space: "The thing I hum appears to be / The rhythm of this celestial pantomime."[80]

The patterns that emerge among things themselves, and among things and the imagination, point toward what Stevens called the central poem. In the created universe, because there is a purpose for the cosmos as a whole, the patterns point to a central poem of the world, the essence that is in-and-beyond existence. If the imagination is a created thing, poetry recapitulates the order of the something more—the transcendent central poem—that fascinated but eluded Stevens. At the limits of our power to communicate our experience of what is ineffable in reality, music orders our words, expressing a kind of spoken–unspoken wisdom in the resonances of our metaphors and the phonic links of our phrases, resonances of the sort that makes us think of the metaphor of a Muse when we encounter true poetry. The Muse knows more than she says. She provokes our souls and stirs us from slumber to coax us into singing a song about the strange realities, visible and invisible, that show up through imagination: "The thing I hum appears to be / The rhythm of this celestial pantomime."

What is the pattern of this central poem? For a theist, the central poem is expressed in the analogia entis, which is fundamentally about the rhythm between God and creation, between the ground and the grounded, between God's scientia visionis that sees through the whole universe and

---

[77] Stevens, „Owl's Clover," 154.
[78] Stevens, „The Well Dressed Man with a Beard," 224.
[79] Stevens, „Final Soliloquy of the Interior Paramour," 444.
[80] Stevens, „Landscape with Boat," 220.

the potency within ourselves that is an image of this power of God. Patterns of reality and the philosophical imagination that reaches for these patterns are both manifestations of essence in-and-beyond existence: they mirror the central poem, calling to us through the poems that appear on the page while hinting at a limitless poetic background, the myth that delights because it is the very pattern that resounds in all the work of the mind—its movement back and forth between the infinite and the finite, the necessary and the contingent, the universal and the particular. It is a kind of play that borrows from the deep structures and mystery of analogy. It must be seen to be seen, like a poem, or a joke, or Anselm's idea of God. We either get it or we do not. Our experience of the infinite, the universal, and the transcendent is not entirely out there. It arises from the peculiar particularities of our local, contingent, fragile individual existence. There is something inside our frailty that must reach toward the transcendent, not in a way that diminishes the value of the immanent but as a genuine expression of our longing for reality. Some part of us is transcendent, and we are made more real by this elusive transcendence. Stevens believe in a relationship between the great fiction of the central poem and its lesser manifestations in imitative poems. In that relationship there is an imaginative space for the idea of transcendence: the play between the central poem and lesser poems is a kind of image of the human mind, the mind of creatures who shine forth the *imago dei*. This idea certainly makes more sense if God exists. It is serious play, and it shines the beam on something that is central to the question of philosophical imagination in a created universe, the relationship of the made to the unmade, the poetic apriori.

Human beings live at the nexus of this paradox between infinite and finite, absolute and contingent, universal and particular. We live in the gap, and our minds are constituted by the prods of these electric charges of metaphysical energy that provoke and sometimes torment us. Because of this, we track down the answers to questions about the unknown by following the ancient philosophical injunction, know thyself. In part, we understand our mysterious minds and our relation to the unknown through what make, the poems that emerge from our minds, as though the work of thinking should be accompanied by the chant, *Bubble, bubble, toil and trouble* ... We search our poems for clues, patterns, and maps that help us see the whole of reality. Imagination is the power that keeps our minds from descending into Earth or flying away into formal abstraction. Imagination keeps us on the bridge between the divine and the world of larval worms crawling through dirt. Imagination keeps our souls grounded in the soil.

What is most valuable about us does not show up in the quantitative measurements of our biology, nor in the metrics of our productivity in the workplace but in the forms of love, play, and sometimes offhanded imaginative expressions that lend flavor to the way we tell the story of our lives to others. It is what shows up in our commitment to a promise, lament over loss, and questions we feel while looking at the night sky. It is what Hopkins called inscape, when we turn toward our own inner reality and our inner experience of outward reality. We discover the value of the cosmos within our imaginations. We value it because it is actually valuable. It makes us happy that the world exists. It makes us ask, Why is there something rather than nothing? and the correlative questions, Why am I something rather than nothing? and Why am I here? These questions provoke our interest in structures of meaning. We want to know whether the scaffolding on which all expression of human meaning hangs is completely of human making or whether that scaffolding depends on resonant structures in the universe that are harmonious and interpretive. If such structures exist, our own sense makes deeper sense. They locate the fragments of our contingent lives within the whole, orienting the stuttering brokenness of our minds to the mind beyond mind that allows stillness even on the threshold of our own graves. Stevens rejected this possibility, not because he did not desire it and not because the patterns in mind and in the world failed to move him to wonder about God but simply because he could not, or would not, have faith, whatever that means.

So, which view of reality is truer? If a poem is proved only by another poem, how do we climb the ladder of poems to reach the central poem, the source of whatever reality poetry has? This is a shadow of the questions about ourselves and the world. Are we disconnected finite selves in a universe of disconnected finite things? Are we finite contingent selves fundamentally separated from the absolute? Are we contingent selves that are somehow related to the absolute but in a way closer to the analogia entis of the Catholic and Eastern Orthodox traditions? Are we isolated finite contingent beings who can choose for our connections with other people to be profoundly meaningful and just as easily choose to hook up casually, and by merely proclaiming the relationship to be casual, make it so? Or do we connect to each other within a larger frame of meaning that is not merely immanent but that has a transcendent relation defining the meaning and consequence of the union? We can ask questions about human transactions that require trust, form minds, create culture, and change our bodies. But perhaps none of these has the implications of the singular union found in sex, not merely because of how it involves our bodies and not merely because it can lead to the existence of a new human being but also because, well, it is a mystery, and it feels important.

Those of us who love reality want to be fully ourselves. But our search meets with paradoxes to which both the mystics and the poets bear witness. There are echoes in Stevens of the mystic's insight in his poem "The Idea of Order at Key West": "The glassy lights, / The lights in the fishing boats ... / Mastered the night ... / Fixing emblazoned zones ... / Arranging, deepening, enchanted night." The light makes the dark darker, makes it more itself. Following Hopkins, we might borrow the language of Scotus to say that the thisness of the light deepens the thisness of the dark, without becoming the dark. Through the one, we see the other more clearly. The analogia entis functions in this way, as the form of our insight into the imago dei. Analogy also reveals the distance between creator and creature, which is the condition for creaturely existence as a gift from God. Simone Weil gestured toward this when she wrote about the absurdity of our life: "Everything that we want is in contradiction with the conditions or consequences which are attached to it. It is because we ourselves are a contradiction, being creatures, being God and infinitely other than God."[81]

From inside the world of science, there are thinkers who bear witness to something similar regarding the deep structures of reality. When we release our diminished view of reality, we begin to discover true things about ourselves by emptying ourselves. But if science becomes one more of our imaginatively cramped idols, it can halt our growth. The pioneer in quantum physics, Erwin Schrodinger, is worth quoting at length to make the point:

> The scientific picture of the world around me is very deficient. It gives me a lot of factual information, puts all our experience in a magnificently consistent order, but is ghastly silent about all that is really near to our hearts, that really matters to us. It cannot tell a word about the sensation of red and blue, bitter and sweet, feelings of delight and sorrow. It knows nothing of beauty and ugly, good or bad, God or eternity. Science sometimes pretends to answer questions in these domains, but the answers are very often so silly that we are not inclined to take them seriously. Science is reticent too when

---

[81] Simone Weil, *Gravity and Grace*, trans. Emma Crawford and Marion von der Ruhr, Routledge Press, New York (1999), xxvi.

it is a question of the great unity of which we somehow form a part, to which we belong. The most popular name for it in our time is God, with a capital "G." Science is, very usually, branded as being atheistic. After what we have said this is not astonishing. If its world picture does not even contain beauty, delight, sorrow, if personality is cut out of it by agreement, how should it contain the most sublime idea that presents itself to the human mind?[82]

Schrodinger's recognition that our minds have such an idea and that this idea is important for our grasp of reality is in the spirit of Anselm whose *Proslogion* was itself an insight into the believing mind. It is the sense of an eternal harmony grounding the music we create, an echo of something fitting to us but residing beyond what can be measured by the wonderful disciplines of science that show us so much about the created world. This is the nature of Stevens's central poem, though he did not believe in a universe in which it could be more than a fiction. The myth of the central poem clears room for the same illuminating disorientation that occurs whenever the transcendent breaks in on the predictable, controllable, stable world of our daily life. It gives us a taste of what we call—using a placeholder in the face of the unsayable—heaven. The unifying argument from experience turns on the reality of beauty, which is ineffable but which shows up by its very nature.

The poet, like all of us at our best, seeks to make a bridge between what is real and what is made in the cauldron of our own living imaginations, rooted in lives that must hold together everything from sexual union, to tying our shoes, to craving spiritual answers when our world is breached or fractured. New fractures occur, sometimes on the heels of unwieldy questions, and the unity that we crave eludes us, tipping over the horizon of this curved existence. Stevens's man with the blue guitar says, "I cannot bring a world quite round, / Although I patch it as I can." In saying this he speaks for us, whether we believe that our only tools for patching are fictions all the way down or else believe there is more to the story. Of course, we know we do not know everything. But the story of what we know evolves as our imaginations reach farther and as we talk among ourselves about what we discover. Great poetry reveals a suggestive pattern recurrent in the best efforts of the mind and imagination—in mathematically describable motions of the planets and subatomic particles, eruptions of metaphysical systems, proportions incarnate in great cathedrals and works

---

[82] Erwin Schrodinger, *My View of the World*, Cambridge University Press, Cambridge (1964), 93.

of art, and in the never adequately accounted for splay of beauty everywhere. Such poetry is a portrait of the journey of our minds and imaginations in this short life.

Stevens was pessimistic about our sense of having a telos, an end that is more than a fiction. Hopkins caught a glimpse of something more, like God passing by Moses and covering his eyes, allowing him to see only his back. It is worth remembering that the reason God allowed Moses to see only his back was that anyone who sees the face of God must die—or to say it a different way, we must die to see the face of God. In "Sunday Morning" Stevens writes, "She says, 'But in contentment I still feel / The need of some imperishable bliss.' / Death is the mother of beauty; hence from her, / Alone, shall come fulfillment to our dreams / And our desires …"[83] The relationship between death and seeing the face of God extends to our attempts to express the ineffable, to whatever exists before all our making, which we discover through the imaginative work of the poetic apriori.

Meanwhile we are alive, and we seek the face of God, whether as a fiction or as a way to worship better. The elusiveness of that face comes from its distance, the interval that is necessary for our own existence, a loving withdrawal that is a condition for creation. But as we imagine the truth of the invisible, we can also wonder whether this elusiveness of God's face comes in part because God's face is changing. Do our acts of creation make us partners in the process that is the making of God? The idea of the poetic apriori presses this question above all: What is this invisible that is revealed and betokened by the leaf and the blade of grass, presented to a mind with an imagination capable of seeing the poetry of the world?

---

[83] Stevens, „Sunday Morning," 55.

VIII. Imagination and Partnership with God to Create a World

In his poem "Negation" Stevens wrote: "Hi! The creator too is blind, / Struggling toward his harmonious whole ..."[84] This could have been the epigraph for Alfred North Whitehead's book, *Adventures of Ideas*, and indeed his entire life's work. Whitehead knew that when we tell stories about the world and stories about the history of our storytelling about the world, we always do so from the particular viewpoint of a mind. Stories can have no other starting point.[85] But he believed that our deepest stories, far from being transient fictions, might be part of the process we call the creation of the world. His central question was this: Is the process of creation one in which God struggles alongside us toward a harmonious whole? If so, this would have profound consequences for the role of imagination in making the world we experience.

The human mind experiences reciprocity between the act of contributing to the reality of the world and the act of grasping notions about the world that do not yet fit our language. Apprehension comes to us slowly, and the purpose of philosophy is to nurture this kind of growth in our minds.[86] Good philosophy remembers its own history, delving into the easily forgotten starting points of thought in the imaginative life of the human mind. In one sense, the history of ideas that have emerged from the human mind is a history of mistakes. We no longer accept Jove as an explanation for thunder, and we have very good reasons to think that our current meteorological explanation of thunder is superior, assuming it is thunder we wish to understand. But if we want to understand the reality of the human mind and imagination, then the history of mistakes is not merely a museum of human foibles: it is a clue to the patterns of forces to which the mind responds. The mistakes the imagination makes reveal something about both the mind and the reality to which the mind responds.

The myth of Jove might not be the best way to understand thunder, but it is an important part of understanding minds of the sort that drift to-

---

[84] Wallace Stevens, *Collected Poetry and Prose*, ed. Frank Kermode and Joan Richardson, Library of America, New York (1997), 82.
[85] Alfred North Whitehead, *Adventures of Ideas*, Free Press, New York (1967), 4.
[86] Whitehead, *Adventures*, 24.

ward the divine when trying to explain reality. Memory links the imaginative stages of the mind's evolution. Without memory, our gains are accompanied by losses that leave us with a very partial view of mind and reality, threatening a return to the barbarism Vico predicted. Imagination is not a ladder to be kicked away after we have ascended to the height of philosophical abstraction and the world of the intelligible universal. Religion is the most powerful arena in which the imaginative universal and the intelligible universal are held in one mind and, collectively, in a tradition that views the world through the lens of the analogia entis. But the move from temporal fact to eternal greatness, from the finite to the infinite, from the imaginative universal to the intelligible universal, requires its own kind of discernment and attentiveness to avoid spinning into nonsense. Metaphysical clarity is required to resist sophistry in our movement from one to the other and back again.

We are tempted to call our working intellectual systems complete. But wisdom leads us toward honesty about gaps in our understanding. This honesty is essential if we wish to deepen our understanding of the world. The omissions in our systems of thought are important. They can be filled in through experimentation, exploration, and imagination. But we obscure their importance if we resist surprise and uncertainty and attempt to preserve the illusion of completeness in our understanding of the whole. Claims to certainty close off possibility. This is not always a bad thing: when we have to act definitively in the moment, bracketing epistemological concerns can be pragmatic, allowing us to treat diseases, build cities, and fly to the moon. But as a way of framing the mind's relationship to reality, it is stultifying and arrogant. Whitehead insisted that a so-called hard-headed clarity covers over the complexities we encounter in the real world. It stems not from intellectual integrity but rather from a kind of sentimental feeling: "Insistence on clarity at all costs is based on sheer superstition as to the mode in which human intelligence functions. Our reasonings grasp at straws for premises and float on gossamers for deductions."[87]

These gossamer links require the imagination, if not as a final destination then at least as a tether to aspects of reality that lie outside our current knowledge or even farther, to realms in which we do not yet know that we do not know. Newton did not know that he did not know quantum mechanics. Heraclitus did not know that he did not know about the

---

[87] Whitehead, *Adventures*, 72.

analogia entis. Persuasion, not force, is how civilization is built, but accepting this requires humility. If we use our partial knowledge to silence other voices, we denigrate our own minds and imaginations, and our intellectual and imaginative lives become a repetition of familiar maxims, formulas, and false absolutes. Wielding a narrow knowledge to silence others is a philosophic habit that can lead to power of a certain sort, but it is devastating and world-shrinking. We should resist it, even though at points in history resisting it has led to death. Philosophy has its martyrs who died for the sake of imagination. Socrates was one. Bruno was another.

Whitehead was concerned about the effects of an unimaginative truncation of the mind's activity. He worried this might blind us to parts of reality. Unlinking imaginative reach from critical thought denigrates both. It thins our view of reality. It makes us timid and narrows our scope of inquiry to trivialities, while relegating the remainder of experience to religion and mysticism, construed as inferior to the certainties of desiccated scholarship: "The world will again sink into the boredom of a drab detail of rational thought, unless we retain in the sky some reflection of the light from the sun of Hellenism."[88] The extent to which the mind determines the brightness of this light and the conditions necessary for a mind to experience such light are open questions. Timidity is the target of Whitehead's criticism. Self-aware honesty about the sources and manifestations of our own timidity are prudent safeguards against it. We may even be required to take seriously the perspectives of those who understand the practices of religion and mysticism.

Nor will a retreat into probabilities allow us to escape imaginative modes of thought. Our probabilities rest on assumptions that only our philosophical imaginations can provide. At the very least, we must assume the stability of statistical form. After David Hume, inference from probability to concrete facts in the natural world is anything but obviously valid. And because we only have direct access to the surface of one planet, our reach toward nature is severely restricted. We embrace the metaphor of natural laws in faith as we try to hone our observations and explanations of the natural world. It is an excellent faith to hold, because this is the only way we can study the natural world. But we must take care not to lose other kinds of knowledge, including the kinds of philosophical knowledge that form the foundation for the science. Even worse is to lose such insight and then to make a virtue of the loss by insisting that what remains is the only

---

[88] Whitehead, *Adventures*, 118.

legitimate form of knowledge. A failure to be curious about other ways of knowing is a failure to be curious about reality. Fortunately, such imaginatively limited views of knowledge and insight have always crumbled, even if they periodically attempt to reemerge. Science and philosophy provide each other with imaginative resources. There is a reciprocity between the reach of scientific method and the metaphorical presumptions upon which such advance is founded. This reciprocity is needed to avoid the collapse of both reason and imagination. This is the only way we can throw the dart beyond the bounds of the world, to use Lucretius's metaphor. Truly creative discovery in the world requires "the throbbing emotion of the past hurling itself into a new transcendent fact."[89]

As things and ideas emerge in reality, they struggle for existence beyond themselves. The struggle occurs in conditions that neither guarantee nor fully determine their emergence. Even when an appearance emerges from so-called reality, there is no metaphysical principle accounting for the ways in which appearance and reality differ. A change in the social context in which our minds are embedded can change our sense of what is real and what is appearance. Reality and appearance might seem to merge in conditions of stability over time, but our perspective on reality and appearance is never some ideal form of knowledge without a knower. It is deeply informed by memory and imagination, both of which recollect the past in the form of stories that provide our starting points for hurling into the as-yet unknown. New discoveries float into the past, becoming in turn the inescapable condition for our next adventures.

The living body—with a brain that is continuous with the body, which in turn is continuous with the world—is the organ for all experience in the world. This is not incidental. We navigate a complex and interactive reality, and we tell each other about what we find as we stretch past familiar outposts and boundaries. Religion, literature, science, and philosophy all attempt to discover ways to express meanings that have not yet been expressed.[90] Our regulative appraisal of these expressions leads us to retain certain ideas and to emphasize certain ways of expressing the truth we find in experience. Truth refers to the conformation of appearance to reality, whether we are referring to the truth of our senses, which is the culmination of appearance for many animals, or the truth of a proposition.

---

[89] Whitehead, *Adventures*, 177.
[90] Whitehead, *Adventures*, 227.

Propositions are truth-relations that have a peculiar place in Whitehead's thought: "It is more important that a proposition be interesting than that it be true. This statement is almost a tautology, for the emerging of operation of a proposition in an occasion of experience is its interest and its importance. But of course a true proposition is more apt to be interesting than a false one."[91] Whitehead's own quote demonstrates the principal. Some of the most interesting propositions arise from a necessarily vague kind of truth that he calls symbolic truth, which includes music, ceremonial clothing, ceremonial smells, and ceremonial rhythmic visual appearances, along with languages and their meanings. In these cases, vagueness can be a virtue.

Whitehead believed the cosmos is moving toward an end, with a strange teleology aimed at bringing about beauty. I am not sure that his definition of beauty—perfection of harmony defined in terms of perfection of subjective form in detail, and final synthesis and strength—adds much to the value of his insight. But there is a compelling and intriguing resonance between his convictions about the telos of the universe and those of Aquinas, for whom a thing is good insofar as it is and for whom beauty, truth, and goodness are intimately related. For Whitehead, the goodness of truth is inseparable from its beauty.[92]

When meaning and fact are attached to each other, the attachment occurs in consciousness. This is especially true for art, in which the artist's consciousness aims for truthful beauty by adapting appearance to reality. Art is essentially artificial, but it is most fully itself when it approaches nature while still remaining art: "Art is the education of nature. Thus, in its broadest sense, art is civilization. For civilization is nothing other than the unremitting aim at the major perfections of harmony."[93] Whitehead combines Aristotle's idea that art imitates life, and Oscar Wilde's converse belief that life imitates art. The reciprocity between the idea that art educates nature, and the idea that it is perfected by approaching nature, feels similar to Stevens's idea that poetry adds to the *res*. But where Stevens's artifacts constitute a supreme fiction, for Whitehead there is a notion of harmony, beauty, and direction to the universe that provide some measure for the value of what is made. The imagination certainly makes fictions, but there is a reality to which the fiction may or may not conform. For

---

[91] Whitehead, *Adventures*, 244.
[92] Whitehead, *Adventures*, 267.
[93] Whitehead, *Adventures*, 271.

Whitehead, this conformation bears upon its value in the life of the mind and soul, in a way that it cannot in the supreme fiction of Stevens's world.

When we create a poem, a story, or a system of metaphysics, we are aware that we are consciously creating something. But as we observe ourselves making something, we are also aware that our consciousness grows through a non-conscious, or a partially conscious, or an other-than-conscious operation that is imagination—the power of genuine discovery through play. When we pay attention to our own imaginative work, we gain knowledge about ourselves, and we gain insight into the ways reality might be changed through our perception of it. Our fallible perception can introduce refractive error, but insofar as it is reality bumping up against us, our lenses might also be improved and our vision made truer. In a created world, it is possible to believe the creator intends for us to grasp reality in an ever-deeper way, even if the word intend is a placeholder for *we know not what*, a placeholder for something we can reach only by analogy.

One mark of civilization is the growing capacity of philosophical imagination to accommodate ever-larger and more general ideas, including ideas related to quality, importance, and fact—that a thing is, what a thing is, and what the value of a thing is. Whitehead's understanding of process expresses the idea of importance in its most general form. Morality, logic, religion, and art are species of importance.[94] Process is not restricted to any single category of expression—morality, logic, religion, art—but is formed by the whole force of what we call reality, within which importance is manifested. Because the contours of importance are shaped by reality, philosophy must rise out of the perceptions and assumptions of ordinary life, where social relations emerge. Civilization is a kind of instrument for perceiving reality, within which wisdom reveals itself through the artifacts imaginative creatures make. Critical thought must begin with what actually shows up in the world if our philosophy is to remain tethered to reality.

Our lived experience begins with that part of the world we call our bodies. We feel with our bodies. History is a record of what we feel as our relationships with reality change. We must maintain openness to possibility to grow in our knowledge of reality as relations shift in the networks of the world, language, body, mind, and soul. Otherwise, we retreat to the safe havens of what we think we already know or else we distill away the mystery and strangeness of things into calculable abstractions that reside

---

[94] Alfred North Whitehead, *Modes of Thought*, Free Press, New York (1966), 11.

in an ever-diminishing space we call intellect. Philosophy is diminished when it timidly limits itself to relationships it can manage while rejecting the growing edge of our intimacy with new aspects of reality, which often feel vague in the beginning. Condescension toward the instability of new, as-yet dimly perceived ideas about reality is closer to cowardice than intellectual integrity.

As we acquire language to tell others about the discoveries our imaginations make within ordinary experience, we develop a collective intelligence, which we can analyze to improve our understanding of the world. Anything that exists is knowable, but the whole will always be greater than our own finite knowledge. The infinity of the whole, though comprehensible in each of its parts, is forever beyond the totality of our knowledge. Thomas conceived of God in a similar way—profoundly comprehensible in one sense but incomprehensible in another sense, because of our finitude. Such humility is central to Whitehead's posture toward the philosophical imagination. We are, by our very natures, creatures who are on the way. At the edge of imagination's reach, we delve into a past that is recollected, a present that appears fleeting, and a future that has yet to be made. This is essential to the nature of creatures such as ourselves, swimming in a vast reality that existed before us, and always falling short as we try to express what we discover about it.

When we do try to say something about the world, disclosing the contents of our minds, the contents become manageable. Saying things allows us to connect otherwise fragmentary inklings. But sometimes the connections we make through language may not exist in reality. This is why we must question so-called proofs in philosophy. We make intellectual abstractions and use them to construct philosophical proofs. Our only test for the truth of our proof is either the self-evident nature of our abstractions or else a return to unabstracted reality. But we never return to some primal version of reality, because expressing and analyzing the contents of our minds changes the way we see the world. Philosophy wants to disclose reality, but it must do so with a language that can distort reality. The biggest failures of philosophy are failures of language, but because of the kind of creatures we are, this is our only way into reality.[95]

In philosophy and poetry, our language is always outrun by our intuitive and imaginative encounters with reality. We know more than we can say, and to say more of what we know, we must learn to use language

---

[95] Whitehead, *Modes of Thought*, 48.

in new ways. If we believe there is order at the foundation of reality, which is an act of faith, it is reasonable to believe that sharing what we discover through imagination can lead to truer perceptions of reality. Saying what we discover helps us to see, as much as seeing helps us to say things. But along the way, we will encounter apparent inconsistencies. We can either dismiss these inconsistencies, to maintain the integrity of our intellectual systems, or we can tarry with inconsistency, hoping to discover a deeper consistency. Our philosophical imaginations cannot grow if we always exclude inconsistencies. Whitehead conceives of process as the mechanism for avoiding such exclusions.[96]

Inconsistency can be logical or aesthetic. Logic focuses on abstraction. Logical inconsistencies occur among abstracted things in a set of ideas we are analyzing for pattern and fit. Aesthetics stays closer to the concrete. The distance between the abstract and the concrete constitutes the difference between logic as a function of the understanding and aesthetics as a function of the understanding. Both are needed by a finite mind that tries to grasp the infinite, disclosing what is closed to us. Disclosure is the central act of the soul wandering the cosmos. This is why our philosophical style is not an esoteric activity reserved for experts but rather is at the heart of living and thinking about the reality in which we work, love, and make civilization.

We can talk abstractly about reality apart from our perception of it—reality is everything that is real, and everything that is something is real. But if we are going to talk about reality as we perceive it, we must talk about modes of reality and the relationships among modes of reality. We only have access to the world as it discloses itself to us in experience, through our peculiar modes of knowing. But we can grow in our ability to experience and to know. Philosophical imagination can go beyond questions about modes of knowing and speculate on modes of reality to which we might aspire, once we catch a glimpse of them. Three pairs of opposites allow us to establish principles of division in experience: clarity and vagueness, order and disorder, and good and bad. Each of these is related to form as it shows up in the world. Form requires limitation, finitude. It has a boundary, beyond which extends everything that is not the form. Our minds have a peculiar and wonderful ability to extend imaginatively beyond the limitations of form to the idea of infinity. We can perceive the

---

[96] Whitehead, *Modes of Thought*, 54.

relation of a particular form to the remainder of reality, known and unknown, knowable and unknowable. Our capacity both to perceive form and to grasp infinity leads to our sense of importance in the universe.[97]

Our discovery of order is always incomplete because it is linked to the limits of possibility determined by our bodily existence. Dissatisfaction with incompleteness is part of what motivates our intellectual and imaginative adventures. Our grasp of the whole is limited by our own finitude, and our comprehension of even the most familiar aspect of our universe is always partial. But process, in Whitehead's sense, provides a rhythm of discovery in which we discern, however vaguely, the contours of individual things and facts. These always remain part of an infinite interconnected universe beyond us, and things that appear to us as discrete facts can never be abstracted from process without losing their meaning. Individual things have their meaning only in relation to process. Our contribution to creation lies in this: process has no meaning apart from the perspectives on the universe brought into being by all individual things. Time allows the movement of meaning, hope, fear, and energy. Space allows the consummation of an individual existing thing. Together, time and space allow the realities of transition and achievement that are aspects of process. Finally, the divine enables the universe to take on importance, value, and ideals it would not have otherwise. We struggle to grasp what has come before, what shall come in the future, and what the meaning of reality is. Philosophical imagination begins in wonder and reaches for new horizons, but completeness will always elude us, goading us onward.

Onward toward what? Toward the discovery of reality conceived as valuable and meaningful. Discovery requires that reality be viewed in this way, because apart from meaning and value, no goal is worth pursuing. Dead, meaningless nature cannot aim for anything, because it cannot value anything.[98] Modernity combined the mechanics of Newtonian physics, in which the world yields no reasons, with Hume's interpretation of data, which offers no meaningful causal relationships among events in the world. From this came a philosophy incapable of making the world intelligible beyond matters-of-fact that occur in an instant, excluding other modes of understanding oriented toward intuition, insight, and meaning.

---

[97] Whitehead, *Modes of Thought*, 78.
[98] Whitehead, *Modes of Thought*, 135.

This interrupts philosophical speculation before it even begins, and it undercuts our attempts to discover interconnections in the cosmos, even when asking the most basic questions of science.

Because of the way science has developed, it is incapable of acknowledging aims or creativity in nature and instead discovers mere rules of succession. Descartes's separation of the mind and body in his philosophy is at the root of this unfortunate history. The separation of the body from the mind requires that we also set aside the world of emotion, all of which is either derived from or modified by the body. This separation had a devastating effect on the way we value mental experience, including the ways we feel for meaning in a living philosophical act. We must overcome this if philosophy is going to aim at grasping the transcendent aspect of reality that is the condition for our experience of value, meaning, and direction. Even when philosophy has done its best work, we still experience the incompleteness of our grasp, and we see the true proportions of a reality that is always beyond us. Philosophy is akin to mysticism in its reach for insight into the as-yet unknown. It is also akin to poetry in its search for a language to express our discoveries in this immense and strange universe.

Einstein led scientists to move from theories in which the universe is made up of particles to theories in which everything is made of fields. From there, many scientists moved on to the idea that everything, in so far as it has a form, is information that precedes the manifestation of the thing in matter. This development in scientific thinking suggests ways we might reframe our experience of the universe, as well as our experience of our own minds as they experience the universe. If information precedes material expression, we can entertain the astonishing possibility that the first time a bird sang, it was not merely atoms gone crazy for a moment but was actually a bird singing—a new thing in the world. Among the things in the universe, we have unique access to the way that our minds work with different kinds of information, and in our own experience intelligence is the ground of true information. We also know that imagination brings forth new things in the mind, bound only by the strictures of possibility. Whether we are talking about birds, ideas, or stories, we must return to questions about the foundation and meaning of information in our universe. Discoveries in science compel us to rethink our relationship to this unfolding reality and the peculiar place of the mind in this world.

In his Gifford lectures, published as the book *Process and Reality*, Whitehead used the lens of speculative philosophy to focus on relationships within human experience. From the start he acknowledged the incompleteness of his own theory, because we lack the insight and language necessary for any set of complete metaphysical first principles. Metaphysical principles, whatever their value, can appear to have an artificial and deceptive stability. But for Whitehead, all metaphysical principles, including his own, are little more than "metaphors mutely appealing for an imaginative leap."[99]

Any growth in our understanding, including our scientific understanding of the world, requires imagination. The inductive method introduced by Francis Bacon and embraced by empiricists would lead nowhere apart from imagination. This work of the mind—constructing ideas that move back and forth between experience and imagination, seeing the world under the influence of imagination in an effort to understand reality—has room for disagreement, and even inconsistency, among possibly true ideas. But it also trusts in the value of returning to experience and critique and understanding advances only if the play of imagination is free of contradiction. As imaginative constructions unfold, their success depends on their relationship to human interest. They must be logical and coherent, which is simply an expression of faith in order. Logic and coherence are the internal conditions of language and rational life, but the premises from which rational thought proceeds depend upon imaginative insights that transcend the familiar, the obvious, and the accepted.

Imagination is formed in the atmosphere of a rational life, and as it enlarges the mind's awareness of forces at work in reality, it expands the language available to rational thought. Ficino's magical practices—with his poetic and musical incantations and his use of magical images—were aimed at conditioning the imagination to receive celestial influences. Likewise, if any creative metaphysics is going to understand the complex operations of language in the development of philosophy, it must consider the forces that create a language and the civilization in which a language lives. Reality will always be larger than the language available to philosophy. This means that imaginative leaps will always be required for progress. The elasticity of the imagination allows our minds to create schemas of reality and to adapt to reality as our schemas grow. Imagination is the mind's potential for deepening reason in ways that reason cannot guess,

---

[99] Alfred North Whitehead, *Process and Reality*, Free Press, New York (1978), 4.

thereby intensifying sense. The imagination expands through experimentation and philosophical analysis but also through love, feeling, prayer, and storytelling, among many other human acts that are meaningful. The growth of rational thought begins with particular topics, generalizes from them, and then imaginatively schematizes the generalization, comparing the result of this imaginative work to ongoing direct experience. These specialized schemas have a reciprocal relationship with the common sense that emerges within civilizations. Each modifies or provides conditions for the other, and each provides a kind of restraint on the other. Imagination tethered to humanity's common sense, and disciplined by the requirements of logical coherence, creates the pattern of a cosmos from disjointed facts. This is the nature of meaningful philosophical activity, and it is a process of genuine discovery, though our accounts are always asymptotic and incomplete.[100]

A thing is more than its form. Forms participate in things, giving them—things, facts—their definition, their definitiveness. Things and facts are creatures, but they do not exhaust the creativity that allows them to emerge. This creativity is a force that moves from disjunction to conjunction, leading ultimately to the whole that we call the universe. Whitehead's concept of process is just this—the becoming of actual entities in the movement of this ultimate principle of creativity. The unity of a thing is a felt reality, a mode of experience that cannot be dismissed without diminishing our mind's ability to discover what is real. Relevant and illuminating feeling can come in the surprising forms of jokes, horror, disgust, or indignation. In the course of moving from the incoherence of distinct disjunctive facts to the coherence of conjunction in a universe, the way we tell others about our experience leads to and shapes further insights into the truth of the cosmos.

Advances in knowledge have led some to propose a view of the universe that resonates with Plato's idea of eternal forms that determine the nature of temporal things in the world. Einstein, for example, said, "Certain it is that a conviction akin to religious feeling, of the rationality or intelligibility of the world, lies behind all scientific work of a higher order ... This firm belief, a belief bound up with deep feeling, in a superior mind that reveals itself in experience, represents my conception of God."[101] Change in the world, the growth of experience, and the mind's grasp of

---

[100] Whitehead, *Process and Reality*, 17.
[101] Albert Einstein, "Scientific Truth," in *The World as I See It*, John Lane, London (1935), 131.

order and intelligibility in the universe are all emergent. Whitehead conceived of temporal things as arising through their participation in eternal things, with the actual mingling with and emerging from the potential through the mediation of the divine.[102] Plato, Einstein, and Whitehead each had an intuition of a larger order that grounds and frames the world as it shows up in our experience. The most important clue we have about the nature of this ground and frame is the existence of our own minds, which are capable of discovering the intelligibility of reality. We create patterns of possible order, and we test these as lenses on reality, revising them in the course of lived experience. This is how imagination itself grows: insofar as there is a discoverable reality fitting to creatures such as ourselves, this process allows us to see where we have not been able to see before.

The process requires a kind of faith that everything real can find its place in our imaginative schema. Both science and philosophy require this faith to make something of imaginative play that can leap between the Heraclitian idea that all is movement and the Parmenidean idea that all change is illusion. Both ideas, as well as the movement between them, require a foundational principle that provides the limit for acts of the imagination—the principle of non-contradiction. Aesthetic measures such as simplicity and elegance can guide the mind but not with the same sense of necessity as the principle of non-contradiction. It is the basis for all science and philosophy, but it does not necessarily lead us to choose between Heraclitus or Parmenides. Instead, the principle leads us to pursue a view of reality in which each of these contradictory accounts of reality discloses some part of what is true, without breaking on the rock of non-contradiction. Discovery of this sort requires patience, persistence, and even courage, all of which are aspects not of logical compulsion but of virtue. If science and philosophy require this faith, they must also embrace a kind of hope in the possibilities for achieving genuine insight, with a basis for hope that is similar to religion's basis for hope.

The central ontological principle that directs our attention to reality is the conviction that apart from actual entities there is only non-entity, which is to say, nothing; "The rest is silence."[103] Creativity transcends any actuality, and it accounts for its internal constitution. Beyond this, there is only the actuality itself and the experience of the actuality. The reality of the thing unfolds and reveals itself in time. The actualities we experience

---

[102] Whitehead, *Process and Reality*, 40
[103] Whitehead, *Process and Reality*, 43.

in the world are temporal, are not eternal. Insofar as they are both actual and temporal, they had to emerge from a potential. Because a thing has definite form that is different from the forms it might have had, the emergence of an actuality omits other potentialities.

Whitehead distinguished temporal actualities from eternal objects and from God. An eternal object is something that can be conceived without reference to anything in the temporal world that is actual.[104] The primordial nature of God is defined by the fullness of God's conception of eternal objects. The mind of God—speaking analogically, as we must—answers the fundamental requirement that everything must be somewhere, including eternal objects in the general potentiality of the universe. The primordial mind of God provides a place for eternal objects, which Plato intuited in his concept of the world of ideas. The mind of God avoids the incoherent assumption that some explanatory fact can come into the actual world out of non-reality. Actual entities in the actual world are formed from other actual entities. The eternal objects—even if we conceive of them as imaginative placeholders, which apparently Whitehead did not—make it possible for an actual entity to form from other things in the universe. We must approach the idea of eternal objects by beginning with our experience of actual entities. But we cannot give a separate name to every actual entity—every individual tree, every individual animal.[105] Instead, our minds conceive of universals, which are present in things, and which are describable by concepts. These universal concepts can be given names. Underlying both universals and potential things is an extreme, complex continuum that is unified relationally. The continuum is potentiality for division. The division occurs with actual entities. This division, or atomization, of the continuum brings things into time, temporalizes them.

Trouble comes when our post-Cartesian philosophical frames dogmatically truncate the reach of imagination. When we encounter a stone, common sense experiences a definite color and a definite shape perceived as quietly enduring. The stone, so perceived, along with its various relationships of position, dominates our imaginations. The position, shape, and color sometimes change, and the changes are explained by causes, such as the actual entity of a sledgehammer hitting the stone. But if our imaginations go only as far as the quietly enduring stone, with its temporary identity, we get stuck in scientific materialism. This is based upon a mistake—

---

[104] Whitehead, *Process and Reality*, 44.
[105] Whitehead, *Process and Reality*, 52.

the idea that the substance conceived in this way is the ultimate actual entity. We make the same mistake about the stone that we made about the atom. There is a pragmatic usefulness in the idea of an enduring substance with stable qualities, but if we mistake this for the fundamental nature of things, we will fail to discover the truth of the cosmos. Unfortunately, this mistake has been reified in our language and our logic, and this has led to profound errors in our metaphysics that can only be overcome by reimagining our fundamental assumptions about reality.[106]

Descartes, Newton, Locke, Hume, and Kant devised their cosmological theories without recognizing the pervasiveness of this mistake. Plato came much closer to intuiting the truth of reality in the *Timaeus*, as long as it is read as allegory. The world is created as order comes into it: forms enter potentiality and lead to the togetherness that is an actual thing, though not all enduring objects form bodies, as anyone with a mind knows. In the *Timaeus*, the Demiurge gives way to the universal good. Schelling echoed the *Timaeus* when he described God and humanity as evolving out of their common depths, with light and night coinciding, as in the philosophy of Bruno, for whom night was the primal womb of light. Whitehead did not believe in pure chaos, because such a thing is rendered impossible by the immanence of God. But when contrasts between form and chaos are patterned, they can yield depth, resisting the shallowness of experience. Some measure of chaos and vagueness can make harmony more beautiful, so neither should be equated with evil.

Imagination, properly formed, allows us to see patterns where we might otherwise remain blind. David Hume gave one account of how sense perception limits imagination's power. Bare sensation does resist the characteristic nimbleness of imagination. But Whitehead thought Hume exaggerated this weakness and even provided evidence to the contrary when he described imagination's ability to fill in gaps in graduated scales of shades. He also believed imagination found a more hospitable freedom among eternal objects.[107] The individuality that eternal objects lend to what would otherwise be fragments of mere data is the core of his concept of process.

Reality exists in some way apart from our minds, but there can be no knowledge without a knower. Knowledge of ourselves as knowers affects our awareness of what is real. Part of Descartes's monumental discovery

---

[106] Whitehead, *Process and Reality*, 79.
[107] Whitehead, *Process and Reality*, 114.

was his insight into the importance for philosophy of the thinking substance's consciousness of enjoying the experience of consciousness. Beyond our experience of actualities in consciousness, we discover that we can imagine them to be otherwise. This contingency of fact bore in upon Descartes and became the foundation of his method of doubt. It also became his portal for discovery, because our experience of a thing, along with our capacity to imagine it otherwise, reveals a fullness of perception that involves more than mere seeing. It extends to feeling, where we discover the power of the free imagination: we are capable of imaginatively grasping novel concepts that have some kind of reality but that are not yet instantiated anywhere in our experience of the universe.[108] This concept of the imagination keeps our minds from being trapped in the illusion of already-complete accounts of what is real. It allows us to stretch into the realm of possibility where we can find patterns that become our new lenses for seeing things we did not see before. We see back in time when we look up at light from faraway stars. We discover ever-smaller worlds within worlds when we look down through our microscopes. We become aware of emotional and spiritual realities when we look within ourselves.

Whitehead's most radical formulation of his idea that we participate in the process of creation is his subjectivist principle: the universe consists only of elements disclosed in the analysis of the experience of subjects. Apart from the experience of the subject, "there is nothing, nothing, nothing, bare nothingness."[109] If we say that we see a tree, the tree to which we are referring is an interpretation of a tree image. This is the crux of human encounter with reality. It is overwhelming. We cannot take in the whole of reality as it exists or potentially exists. But imagination is the nimblest aspect of our minds, enabling us to travel over the worlds of potentiality and to compared these possibilities with the onslaught of blind experience that dawns as we slowly emerge from mental slumber. The universe is organized in this way, and importance is expressed by what appears to us in this process of organization. When the universe is organized as an object of reason, it is still revisable since reason grows as we exercise judgment about the things we enjoy through the power of imagination.

We make our world, and apart from the world made by our minds, there is nothing for us. But we make our world from reality conceived as

---

[108] Whitehead, *Process and Reality*, 161.
[109] Whitehead, *Process and Reality*, 167.

a whole, which we approach asymptotically. The interface between ourselves and blind experience is imagination. The world is made in our judgment of what imagination serves up to us as potential. All potential is the potential for form, and form is an eternal object. The value of imaginative metaphysical speculation is a value that derives from our attempts to feel for the contours of what is real. This value goes beyond the truth or falsity of any particular theory. Feeling lures us to develop theories about the world, and theory lures us back to feeling. In an intellectual culture that dismisses the importance of this aspect of human experience, the point cannot be overemphasized—the development of good theories about the world requires that we care about what shows up first as feeling. Theories that exclude what is revealed through feeling will eliminate vast swathes of reality, while despising as unserious the deeper ways of seeing the world: "The existence of imaginative literature should have warned logicians that their narrow doctrine is absurd. It is difficult to believe that all logicians as they read Hamlet's speech, *To be, or not to be*, commence by judging whether the initial proposition be true or false and keep up the task of judgment throughout the whole thirty-five lines. Surely, at some point in the reading, judgment is eclipsed by aesthetic delight. The speech, for the theater audience is "…a mere lure for feeling."[110] This is how we say things about the world as a whole. The philosophical imagination erupts in propositions about the world that are meant to do work in our minds. It erupts in a kind of poem.

Propositions are strange entities. They are a hybrid between pure potentiality and actuality. The discipline of logic brings clarity to propositions and to the relations among propositions. But logicians can lose their sense of one of the most important functions of propositions: propositions are a source of feeling. They are a source of feeling not at some high intellectual level, nor at the level of belief, but at the physical level of feeling, part of which resides below consciousness. In their role as originators of feeling, propositions are not tethered to data. This means that propositions may or may not conform to the world, and they may be true, or they may be false. If a proposition that conforms to the world is admitted into feeling, then feeling conforms to fact. But if a proposition that does not conform to the world is brought into feeling, we synthesize something that may or may not bring about order and that may or may not be good. Either way, it is still a novelty, a new form in the actual world.

---

[110] Whitehead, *Process and Reality*, 185.

This is why so much is lost when the function of propositions is construed purely in terms of logic: when propositions do not conform to the world, logic judges them as mistaken, useless, and even harmful. But this completely misses the valuable function of these novel propositions the imagination uses to test patterns, theories, and stories in the world. Error is unavoidable if we want to make novel discoveries in and about the world.[111] We must be willing to play without worrying too much over truth and falsity, at least at the start. Play is crucial for discovery. Imagination is the growing edge of our field of play, in which our desires for truth, beauty, and love lead the mind to create science, philosophy, poetry, and proposals to our beloved, whether we are wooing a lover or wooing a nation through diplomacy. Through imagination we are lured toward a person, an equation, a tree, or a metaphysical feeling. Propositions make the content of these experiences explicit, without regard for the truth or falsity of the propositions nor regard for whether or not the propositions conform to the reality of the world. Judgment is a qualitatively different act by which we decide whether or not to admit these propositions into intellectual belief.

Consciousness awakens when we feel the difference between mere facts in the world and our theories or stories about the world. Insofar as our imagination leads the first march into a theory or story about the world, imagination is necessary for the ongoing development of consciousness. Through acts of the imagination we grow our consciousness of feelings such as horror, relief, and purpose. Feelings entertain propositions, and propositions are in turn lures for feeling. As we become acquainted with this process, we gain a sense of something more, which we are only beginning to feel and which does not easily fit into our language—the deepest lure for feeling that comes from our dawning sense of the nature of God, whether or not we call it God.[112]

Propositions, standing as they do between eternal objects and actual occasions, are always more than what is expressed verbally. Movement between eternal objects and actual occasions occurs within propositions. Our language is inadequate to express this movement without remainder. But our intuitive awareness of this movement motivates our notion of flux—the Heraclitian idea that all things flow. We weave our metaphysical systems around the nidus of this flux. Accounting for flux is one of the

---

[111] Whitehead, *Process and Reality*, 186.
[112] Whitehead, *Process and Reality*, 189.

central purposes of metaphysics. Religious propositions are among the best for expressing our sense of permanence amid change because they bring together the metaphysics of substance and the metaphysics of flux. The contrast between the metaphysical views of permanence and change reveals the contingency of the actual temporal entities that appear in the movement of the flux. The sense of permanence amid change provides the consolation of being created, of being actual, and of being related to eternal objects but not the consolation of stasis at the core of Parmenides's idea of the One. Flux is necessary for creativity because it allows everything that is to have other possibilities, which is both thrilling and terrifying. When feelings emerge, they do so through struggle. Their contingency marks not only what they are but also what they might have been. Every actual entity, though it is a thing with form and felt unity, is also felt as a process, on the way, in passage. An actual entity flows, but it is not all flux, because it is a thing with form related to an eternal object. Propositions express this relationship, but there is always a remainder open to exploration, discovery, and refined expression, moving ever closer to the mark but always falling short.

Propositions reside between eternal objects and actual entities. They provide the imaginative possibilities that allow us as knowers to relate to everything we know and everything we might one day know. To know well and to express what we know is not only to bridge eternal objects and actual entities but also to bridge current experience to the memory of prior experience in consciousness—an insight Plato glimpsed in his doctrine of reminiscence. Our present consciousness illuminates our past experience.

We feel real things in consciousness, and there is a kind of imaginative freedom around the felt thing. Perceptive feelings and imaginative feelings are the two kinds of propositional feelings. We can explore the surroundings of consciousness, but they are not transparently accessible—consciousness is not pure light. The boundaries of consciousness move and are variably blurry, and the light of consciousness waxes and wanes. Clarity of consciousness necessarily correspond to the complexity of complete experience. We can explore the penumbra of consciousness to gain insight and understanding, but the work is always accompanied by uncertainty. We must be willing to suspend judgment rather than prematurely assigning truth or falsity to the patterns we discover. The leading edge of apprehension is an active conscious imagination, the content of which may or may not be true. Imagination takes us to new places in the actual world, but that is not the end of the work.

Our theories are stories into which we gather all that we experience in consciousness. The stories are never static: elements that seem stable can escape into the flux, and within the flux we find things with abiding stability. The skill we use to preserve order in the middle of change must not stifle the imagination's expansion, which introduces change into order as it reaches for novelty. Imagination is how we lean into the less well-lit penumbra of our conscious experience of reality: "Life refuses to be embalmed alive."[113] Imagination's reach is enlivening. It is also be terrifying when novelty threatens the apparent stability of familiar things. But if we want to grow in our discovery of the truth of the cosmos, we cannot escape the various ways permanence and flux manifest in the opposing realities of freedom and necessity, good and evil, and all other forms of the many in the one.

Whitehead's list of contrasts culminates in the contrast between God and the world. Theistic philosophy does not favor political powers, moralistic motives, or distant and abstract deities such as the unmoved mover. These are all more like forces than persons. Theistic philosophy is motivated by operations of love in the world. Love illuminates purpose in the moment. It transcends discrete data and reveals interconnectedness and movement toward an end, holding reality together as a cosmos filled with meaning. God exemplifies the discovery that comes to us through the labor of metaphysics, the lure for feeling, and desire's eternal urge. The world is realized in the unity of God's nature and the transformation of God's wisdom into the actual created world. Love defines the central metaphor that clarifies the nature of God's transformation and growth—infinite patience with the tumultuous world and attentive concern that desires all good things to be nurtured, and none to be lost: "He does not create the world, he saves it: or, more accurately, he is the poet of the world, with tender patience leading it by his vision of truth, beauty, and goodness."[114]

If God is the poet of the world, we should not be surprised if this throws a philosophically interesting light on the poetic excursions of our own imaginations into the as-yet dim hints and clues of the dawning world. However tentative our first glimpse, we make a world to discover the truth of the world. This is the poetic apriori.

---

[113] Whitehead, *Process and Reality*, 339.
[114] Whitehead, *Process and Reality*, 346.

IX. Imagination and Seeing through Naming

T. S. Eliot submitted his dissertation, *Knowledge and Experience in the Philosophy of F.H. Bradley*, to the philosophy faculty at Harvard in 1916, but he never returned to complete the remainder of the requirements for his degree. In 1964, at the urging of his wife, he published it as a biographical curiosity. Despite the title of the book, Bradley was somewhat overshadowed by Eliot's own struggle to reach toward something far beyond the ostensible topic of the dissertation, something he tried to hunt down his entire life. His book is more riff than exegesis on Bradley. Feeling was at the center of what he was doing, and the felt thought was, so to speak, the still point around which everything else moved as he explored what we are to do with the world as it shows up: "There is no greater mistake than to think that feeling and thought are exclusive—that those beings which think most and best are not also those capable of the most feeling."[115] Saying what these feelings are and what they mean is difficult but also important. Eliot knew how hard it was to say what he wanted to say, and he felt justified in using this difficulty as an excuse for those places where he failed to be lucid.[116] This difficulty never left him, and he tried over and over, in various ways, to elucidate the central reality that began to take shape in the dissertation:

> So here I am, in the middle way, having had twenty years —
> Twenty years largely wasted, the years of l'entre deux guerres —
> Trying to learn to use words, and every attempt
> Is a wholly new start, and a different kind of failure
> Because one has only learnt to get the better of words
> For that thing one no longer has to say, or the way in which
> One is no longer disposed to say it. And so each venture
> Is a new beginning, a raid on the inarticulate
> With shabby equipment always deteriorating
> In the general mess of imprecision of feeling,
> Undisciplined squads of emotion.[117]

---

[115] Thomas Stearns Eliot, *Knowledge and Experience in the Philosophy of F.H. Bradley*, Columbia University Press, New York (1989), 18.

[116] Eliot, *Knowledge and Experience*, 100.

[117] Thomas Stearns Eliot, „Four Quartets," *T.S. Eliot: The Complete Poems and Plays*, Harcourt, Brace, Jovanovich, New York (1978), 123. All quotations of Eliot's poetry are from this edition.

Bradley influenced Eliot's poetry and the style of his prose. His idealism was unique. In some forms of idealism, a network creates an object by knowing it (Berkeley), or the act of knowing an object transforms it in a way that creates an unbridgeable chasm between the knower and the thing-in-itself (Kant), or the knower and the known belong to a whole that is an all-inclusive actualization of Geist (Hegel). Bradley rejected these. In his form of idealism, the subject and the object come into existence at the same time within an event. His technical term for this event was experience. Within experience, understood in Bradley's peculiar sense, there is no distinction between subject and object. This wholeness was central to his idealism. Against the backdrop of Bradley's idealism, Eliot set out to investigate whether or not the self can know anything outside itself. The short answer is Yes. But what we can actually know falls short of what we wish to know.

Eliot grappled with the possibility of experiencing the world as a unity, beyond the incremental approach of the fact gatherer and the discursive laborer. Much of his life and art was an attempt to achieve this wholeness. But all around him, and within himself, the world fell into unconnected pieces. He saw a fallen world, but he hoped for a return to the experience of the world as whole. He had no interest in the lure of Cartesian certainty. The crisis in epistemology at the turn of the 20th century ended that seduction for Eliot. His book is about the reasons we cannot construct a view of the world as a whole without faith and goodwill. He used strange language to express this idea, but the language he used was not nearly as strange as the thing he tried to say.

Bradley's idealism illuminates Eliot's conclusions (and perhaps his poetry as well). It avoids the mistake of identifying Eliot as a solipsist; he was not, and he argued vigorously against solipsism. Bradley called his central concept experience, but he used the word in several unique ways. We must understand his (and Eliot's) uses of the word to understand the realities he was naming. There are three kinds of experience. Immediate experience precedes any distinction between the knower and the known, between subject and the object. In immediate experience, knowledge and its object are one. It is a direct experience of knowing and feeling, but it cannot be called mine because this kind of experience is prior to any category called my self. Immediate experience does not belong to a self. It is identified with what Bradley, and Eliot following him, called finite centers. This is a term that is difficult to define, and Eliot's own attempt is a bit enigmatic: "The finite center, so far as I can pretend to understand it, *is* immediate experience."[118] It is the unified whole, prior to the distinction of self from non-self, the whole that will, alas, break up into relational consciousness. But before this dissolving, it just is immediate experience, the only thing that can be called reality. It is close to Vico's idea of the gigante and their imaginative universals. Understanding the idea of a finite center depends upon understanding what immediate experience is.

Immediate experience is the root of the desire to overcome dualism—Kantian or otherwise. It is a direct apprehension of reality as a unity that encompasses the whole but that does not reside in individual consciousness because that would introduce dualisms—mind/matter, knower/known. Immediate experience answers the desire for wholeness, but it is doomed to fall apart because our conscious, self-aware intellects are compelled to organize immediate experience. We separate the conscious intellect from those parts of experience that are not conscious intellect. We parse up experience spatially (here/there), temporally (now/then), ontologically (mind/matter), and epistemologically (knower/known). Unity is lost and the mind is sequestered, abstracted from the unified reality of the whole. From within this partial grasp of reality, we discover the second kind of experience: we appear to ourselves as conscious souls dwelling in a confused and unharmonious world of objects.[119]

How do we find our way back to unified reality if our intelligence is responsible for breaking up immediate experience in the first place? We learned to cure cancer with intelligence. We went to the moon with intelligence. We established civilizations with intelligence. And yet, intellect is the source of disharmony and unreality. Is there any way back to wholeness for intelligent creatures such as us?

There is reason for hope, but achieving the way is difficult for someone rich in intellect—it is easier for a camel to go through the eye of a needle. If there is a way, it is found in the third kind of experience that Bradley and Eliot call transcendent experience. After immediate experience falls apart, the discursive intellect does the work of cataloging fragments and divisions. It then draws lines between the dots in a laborious effort to recover some approximation of wholeness by identifying relationships among discrete things. But the discursive intellect can never achieve unity. In immediate experience, knowing and feeling are joined. After the discursive intellect comes on the scene, the only way back to unity is

---

[118] Eliot, *Knowledge and Experience*, 205.
[119] Eliot, *Knowledge and Experience*, 31.

through transcendent experience in which thinking and feeling are one. Eliot considered John Donne to be one poet who exemplified the ways thought can modify experience, so that thinking is felt. We experience a felt thought:

> Donne, I suppose, was such another
> Who found no substitute for sense,
> To seize and clutch and penetrate;
> Expert beyond experience ...[120]

Discursive intellect lives in a kind of experiential purgatory, always approximating but never reaching the completed end. Transcendent experience converts the discursive intellect, giving it a new purpose and end. The wholeness that was simply present in immediate experience is achieved in transcendent experience as the intellect is made to serve the aim of wholeness by learning to feel thought. Thinking dissolves immediate experience into objects and relations that are unreal. Thinking by itself filters reality, turning it into abstractions that are unreal and bound only by the strings of relations that always fall short of unity. Because of this, thinking always keeps us from reality. We try to get closer. We aim at reality. We pretend to build theories from starting points grounded in experience. We begin with truths to which most people give their assent, and then we try to find novel connections among these truths.[121] But even with all this labor, it is unclear whether or not we can ever achieve transcendent experience. The hope Eliot placed in transcendent experience seemed to diminish over the course of his life, but it was replaced by a different hope.

The object of felt thought is immediate experience, which is always present in the background. We can learn to feel it there. Our hope for achieving wholeness depends on learning to feel this background and then making it an object of thought without refracting it into parts. Because this activity is not itself immediate experience, we will still experience objects in the world as distinct from ourselves and ourselves as distinct from objects. Transcendent experience seems to require that we live among dichotomies, while holding the dichotomous nature of the world in abeyance. We must accept the constructed nature of objects. Naming is constitutive of this middle world, the purgatory of the intellect somewhere be-

---

[120] Eliot, „Whispers of Immortality," 32.
[121] Eliot, *Knowledge and Experience*, 167.

tween immediate experience and transcendent experience. Through naming and the development of language, we develop not only our ideas but our experience of reality as well.

Genesis 2:19 is a story about naming: "Out of the ground the Lord God formed every animal of the field and every bird of the air, and brought them to the man to see what he would call them, and whatever the man called every living creature, that was its name."[122] Eliot echoes this in own account of naming: "Try to think of what anything would be if you refrained from naming it all together, and it will dissolve into sensations which are not objects; and it will not be that particular object which it is, until you have found the right name for it."[123] Apart from the act of naming, we would experience only unbundled sensation, not objects. For an object to be an object, rather than an unstrung series of perceptions, it must retain identity in difference over time. Particular perceptions occur in time, moment by moment. Each moment is unrelated to other moments. The perception, the content of one moment, is related to the content of another moment via the object that endures.

We do not grasp an object through moment-bound particular perceptions. We grasp an object through its name. Without words, no objects.[124] As Wallace Stevens's jar in Tennessee "made the slovenly wilderness surround that hill," our name for an object is the logical and meaning-filled force that organizes our sensations, turning the world of feeling into a world populated by a self and an object. Between immediate and transcendent experience, the world forms only through objects and relations among those objects. Within this world the reality of an object depends upon both the boundary established by naming and the relations the object has to other things in the world. This leads Eliot to conclude that reality is a convention.

If we want to know what an object is, we must know its name. If we want to know whether an object is real or imaginary, we must know its relations. The distinction between the real and the imaginary is not absolute. Far from it. The distinction is always relative to the conventions that constitute our individual experience of reality. Degrees of reality vary depending upon the number and kind of relations that exist. One agonizing variation occurs when an object of desire is possible, and therefore could be real, but is nonetheless imaginary: anyone who has fallen in love but

---

[122] NRSV Genesis 2:19.
[123] Eliot, *Knowledge and Experience*, 134.
[124] Eliot, *Knowledge and Experience*, 132.

been rejected by the beloved will understand this. In the middle world between immediate and transcendent experience, there is no single convention to which reality conforms. Epistemology makes an error when it assumes that the world is a single, complete, consistent reality. The world is full of contradiction and mutually exclusive perspectives, all of which are equally real.

Our true end, in the sense of purpose, is to achieve transcendent experience. It is unclear whether or not we can achieve transcendent experience, but feeling and the life of the mind depend on trying. Because we ate from the tree of knowledge, we live in a fallen world as exiles from the garden. Stevens reconciled himself to this exile through his idea of the Supreme Fiction, but his work had a kind of melancholy since he accepted the Supreme Fiction as fiction. Eliot could not bear this, though he agreed that the philosophy and poetry we make are fictions, insofar as they are never complete. They are never complete in part because we cannot achieve reality and in part because we cannot accept that we cannot achieve reality. When philosophy is doing its work well, it resists our tendency to make premature conclusions about the truth of the world. It is iconoclastic, preventing our pragmatic constructs from becoming idols that interrupt our pursuit of deeper truth. It embraces the practice of questioning our metaphysics so that our metaphysics stays open to new aspects of reality. Eliot concluded his dissertation by writing, "This emphasis upon practice—upon the relativity and the instrumentality of knowledge—is what compels us toward the Absolute."[125] Later in his life he came to believe that we can never reach the Absolute unless the Absolute reaches toward us. He did not want a Supreme Fiction. He wanted a True Myth. And the only True Myth that sufficed for Eliot was Christianity, the story not of humanity reaching the Absolute but of God reaching us.

The philosophical life begins in imagination, it reaches past the stories about the world that are handed to us as children, and it proceeds in light of who we are—fallible creatures who hunger for reality but whose lives are short. Our imaginative journey into reality does not have to go far before we realize that our grasp of truth is never certain, and we have little time to explore and to commit. Given these conditions, we need a few basic starting points upon which to build to flourish. Every account must start somewhere. Wherever we start building our theories, we must always ask,

---

[125] Eliot, *Knowledge and Experience*, 169.

"Is this the reality of *my* world of appearance?"[126] Our acceptance of any metaphysics requires a kind of goodwill. We must assume that truth is one and that reality is one, even if our theory gets it wrong. Metaphysics is a form of play. When we do metaphysics, we pretend our theory is true. But it is only by playing that we feel the contours of reality emerge.

When Eliot converted to Christianity, he found a more satisfying account of what first drew him to Bradley's idealism and the possibility of transcendent experience. The adventure is worthy of a life. Through poetic, philosophical, religious, or scientific acts, we try to glimpse the light, testing the veracity of our discoveries by feeling and thought. But the worlds of Bradley's Absolute and that of Eliot's later Christianity are very different worlds, with very different accounts of thought, feeling, and the act of naming. The kind of universe we live in matters. It determines the meaning of our central imaginative act—naming what shows up in the world. In the myth of creation, where the universe is full of meaning, poetry is the naming of things, a naming that is witnessed and delighted in by the creator.

Though poetry is the act of naming what shows up in the world, it sometimes uses words that are strange to us, or words that are familiar but put to strange uses that awaken our minds. Names remind us of strangeness in a world to which we have grown dull. Strangeness can be overwhelming. Eliot saw this in Coleridge, who was haunted after he was visited by the muse: "He was condemned to know that the little poetry he had written was worth more than all he could do with the rest of his life."[127] The poems of haunted poets leave us wondering whether the haunting is present in the world or only in the poet. Does the poem reveal the haunting or project it? Telescopes are made things, but the mountains we see on the moon are actually there, and we could not see them without the telescope. When a poet names the strangeness of something in the process of creating a poem, our own ability to see can grow as we participate in the poetry. We learn to see the strangeness as more than mere unexpectedness, oddness, or curiosity. It arises from the sense that there is something behind, within, beneath, and above the universe as it shows up for us.

The power of the imagination is transformed within a metaphysics open to wholeness, the Absolute, or God. It becomes a way in. It becomes a way in simply because there is an in to hope for and to pursue through

---

[126] Eliot, *Knowledge and Experience*, 168.

[127] T. S. Eliot, *The Use of Poetry and the Use of Criticism*, Harvard University Press, Cambridge (1961), 59–60.

our poems, stories, music, sculptures, and paintings. When the imagination is baptized in this way, the act of contemplation has both a new partner and new tasks. It has a new partner because the poetic imagination and the philosophical imagination bind themselves to each other. By doing so, both kinds of imagination grow in new ways. It has new tasks because if the poets are saying more than they know, the philosophers have adventures ahead of them they could never have otherwise imagined. That is the best we can do. In the last couple of pages of his book Eliot wrote, "So long as our descriptions and explanations can vary so greatly and yet make so little practical difference, how can we say that our theories have that intended identical reference which is the objective criterion for truth and error? And on the other hand our theories make all the difference in the world, because the truth has to be *my* truth before it can be true at all."[128] But to this we might respond by returning to George MacDonald: "To every person I say, 'Do the truth you know, and you shall learn the truth you need to know'."

In a recent issue of a popular magazine, a prominent cognitive scientist, Donald D. Hoffman, argued that the world we perceive is nothing like reality.[129] Science aims to disclose the nature of reality by disentangling observations from observers. But there are a couple of problems. First, how can a lump of flesh between our ears, obeying the basic laws of the universe, lead to reliable self-conscious experience? Neuroscientists call this the really hard problem. Second, quantum physicists have repeatedly shown that we get our answers wrong if we assume the particles have an observer-independent existence. The physicist John Wheeler has suggested that even though in ordinary circumstances it is useful to say that the world exists *out there*, independent of us, such a theory can no longer be upheld in science. These two problems taken together create a dilemma: neuroscientists struggle to understand how first-person reality is even possible, while quantum physicists grapple with how science can reach anything but a first-person reality.

Hoffman argued that an organism possessing vision tuned only for fitness will always have a survival advantage over an organism that sees reality as it is. He used computer interfaces to illustrate the idea. We see icons on our screens because they have color, position, and shape, which

---

[128] Eliot, *Knowledge and Experience*, 168–69.
[129] Amanda Gefter, „The case against reality," *The Atlantic Magazine*, April 25, 2016.

are the categories we used to navigate the world. But the file on the computer responsible for the icon is nothing like the icon. Likewise, we have been shaped to experience a world that is itself nothing like the complex reality underlying the experience: we avoid picking up snake-shaped things, and avoid stepping in front of train-shaped things. Symbols such as these keep us alive, so we have to take them seriously.

Hoffman calls his theory conscious realism. In this theory, objective reality comprises conscious agents, and only conscious agents. When a person has an operation that splits the corpus callosum, which connects the two hemispheres of our brains, evidence suggests that the person can end up with two separate consciousnesses. But Hoffman's mathematical models also show that when two conscious agents interact, the mathematical structure of the interaction fits the definition of a single conscious agent. We can create new observers by putting separate observers together, and we can do this ad infinitum. Conscious experiences are the most basic ingredients of the world in the theory of conscious realism. They are ontological primitives: the experiences of everyday life—the real feeling of a headache, the real taste of chocolate—comprise the ultimate nature of reality. Much more can be said about what shows up in our experience of headaches and chocolate, along with love, reason, longing, and joy. Hoffmann addresses evolutionary fitness and natural selection, but these mechanisms require a philosophical frame to understand their significance in our world. What kind of universe best accounts for the existence of such experiences?

In the preface to the second edition of *Poetic Diction: A Study in Meaning*, Owen Barfield wrote something that resonates with Hoffmann's work (Barfield wrote the book in 1928 and the preface in 1952):

> Science deals with the world it perceives but, seeking more and more to penetrate the veil of naïve perception, progresses only toward the goal of nothing, because it still does not accept in practice (whatever it may admit theoretically) that the mind first creates what it perceives as objects, including the instruments which science uses for that very penetration. It insists on dealing with 'data,' but there shall be no data given, save the bare percept. The rest is imagination. Only by imagination therefore can the world be known. And what is needed is, not only that larger and larger telescopes and more and more sensitive calipers should be constructed, but that the

human mind should become increasingly aware of its own creative activity.[130]

This creative activity is poesis, and the totality of the mystery within which we show up is the apriori. Imagination is the power that allows us to approach the apriori through our creative making in all its forms. The kind of universe in which we live determines the nature of any correlation between what is revealed in our imaginative contribution to the res, and the remainder of the reality within which we appear. If there is nothing more than the forces of evolution producing maximally fit creatures by natural selection, then we have no reason to think that our creative endeavors have any correlation to the way things really are. If we live in a created universe, it is reasonable to hope that we are always on the way to discovering more and more about the apriori—reality as it is. Embracing either view of the universe is an act of faith.

Our frame affects our ideas of what we are doing when we create something. In *The Republic*, Plato said poets are makers of imperfect imitations of nature, which is itself an imperfect copy of eternal reality. The Neoplatonists thought true artists do not merely imitate nature as it appears but rather imitate an archetypal reality expressed through nature. Barfield borrows from the electrician's world to describe this shift in which "the artist stands, not in series with nature, but in parallel with her."[131]

The idea that art can express archetypes evokes the idea of inspiration. Inspiration can suggest that some mind or spirit possesses the artist. But it can also suggest that an individual artist qua artist is different from the same individual as he or she shows up in day-to-day life. The first kind of inspiration is a passive relation. The second is an active relation connecting the artist and the subject of the art. In one form of inspiration, the artist is taken over by a force or a being, and in the other form the artist produces something in the art that has been grasped through personal effort.[132]

What do poets show us in their poems? What do we learn to see? Human minds have an inside that can be communicated to other minds. Do things in nature have an analogous inside we can learn to see? If we live in a universe of dead matter, upon which the epiphenomena of living

---

[130] Owen Barfield, *Poetic Diction: A Study in Meaning*, Wesleyan University Press, Connecticut (1973), 28.
[131] Owen Barfield, *Speaker's Meaning*, Barfield Press, Oxford (2011), 48.
[132] Barfield, *Speaker's Meaning*, 56.

minds accidentally appear for brief time, we are right to be skeptical about the idea of nature having any sort of inside that resonates—all musical connotations intended—with our own minds. But Barfield believed there is more to a thing than what we can measure. He argued that consciousness evolved from vagueness to a kind of central precision. In this process of evolution, pervasive awareness of our own subjective consciousness has grown through the medium of language, reversing the assumption that matter preceded mind in the history of the universe.[133] Language holds the clues to this evolution of consciousness. The history of this evolution has important implications for our view of the universe.

Language expresses our relationship to the world in a way that reveals something not only about our own minds but also about the world's inherent meaning. We use the objects of the outer world to express elements of our own inner world of thought. We are able to do this, not because these outer objects are mere signs for our own inward impulses, but because they are symbols for our ideas: things represent something besides themselves. The forms in the world are converted by memory into mental images that function as symbols for concepts. This is how language emerges. Language makes abstract thought possible. The symbolic significance in our language is inherent in the forms of the outer world, implying that some metaphors are natural rather than artificial.[134] The fundamental distinction we experience between inner and outer, which allows self-consciousness to emerge from consciousness, results from the symbolizing power that makes language possible. Human beings did not start out as self-conscious beings dwelling in an objective world, trying to make an inadequate copy of the world in their minds. Our subjectivity peeled itself off the world by gradually introducing dualities into the world through language. The evolution of language occurred as part of the process of polarizing the world into inner/outer and subjective/objective. Language gave us the capacity to experience ourselves as on onlookers in the world.[135]

Self-consciousness created a distance between ourselves and nature. It reoriented our minds toward nature, allowing us to acquire the ability to measure, describe, and control it in increasingly clever, useful, and destructive ways. It also blinded us to the meaning of nature, including human nature. Just as understanding a word is different from describing its

---

[133] Barfield, *Speaker's Meaning*, 78.
[134] Owen Barfield, *The Rediscovery of Meaning*, The Barfield Press, California (1977), 19.
[135] Barfield, *The Rediscovery of Meaning*, 20–21.

color and shape, grasping the meaning of a thing is different from measure and manipulating it. But to understand the meaning of a word, one must believe that words have meanings we can discover. Likewise, to read meaning in nature, including our own nature, we need the capacity to register meaning, along with a philosophical frame with room for the possibility that there is something meaningful in nature to be read.

Self-consciousness reveals the threshold between ourselves and nature. It also reveals a threshold within ourselves—an awareness that consciousness is more than self-consciousness and that this consciousness beyond self-consciousness is real and accessible. Acquaintance between Western and Eastern approaches to philosophy, psychology, and religion has deepened exploration of the so-called unconscious mind and the power of the imagination. We have learned more about the difference between an image and that of which it is an image. This difference is also a relationship. The relationship is illuminated by the ancient notion of inspiration, not as some tame version of a vaguely poetic Muse but as "the deadly serious doctrine of mania (divine frenzy, divine possession, *enthusiasmos*) ... something more like what happened to the Cumaean Sibyl before she began to speak to Virgil."[136]

The imagination works at the thresholds between self and not-self, conscious and unconscious, mind and matter, human and divine. If we view the imagination as an isolated, self-involved faculty, creating artifacts that are irrelevant to our discovery of reality, we will never grasp its significance. But once we accept the imagination as a power that allows us to see both sides of these thresholds in our search for the truth of the whole, we will understand how philosophical imagination leads us to a kind of knowledge we can gain in no other way.

We know that practice is required to reach the deep parts of a discipline. We do many mathematical problems before we have minds capable of mathematical discovery. We repeat the experiments of others in the laboratory before we become scientists capable of independent investigation and discovery in the realm of the natural world. The same is true for philosophical imagination, which is developed and strengthened as it learns to use images, metaphors, and symbols. This changes the imagination's relationship to language, as a mathematician's relationship to the order within equations changes with practice and experience. The mind learns how to

---

[136] Barfield, *Speaker's Meaning*, 175.

reach beyond horizons that seemed fixed. It learns to apprehend and express new aspects of reality, including the reality of our own minds.[137] This is what Husserl gestured toward when he described the inexhaustible infinity of apriori in our minds.

Language is the storehouse of the imagination. It mediates the transition from the immersed but unindividualized consciousness—Vico's imaginative universals, Eliot's immediate experience—to the mind capable of self-consciousness and awareness of the world as other than itself. Language carries the history of human consciousness within itself. If we forget the spirit from which language grew, we impoverish it, turning it into manipulative slogans to gain power over others or using it to express mere facts without meaning. When we do this, we cut ourselves off from important kinds of knowledge about ourselves and the world. The stakes are high but the context is as ordinary as daily life, in which our imaginations are empowered by metaphor to experience the world as a world instead of as mere sense data. All meaningful knowledge in and of the world comes to us through analogy. Apart from the imagination's power of analogy and metaphor, we are left only with unconnected facts and data, rather than a cosmos that hangs together.[138]

In Vico's theory of the imaginative universal, the theological poets did not have the power of abstraction. The poetic wisdom by which they ordered, named, and navigated the world expressed a kind of metaphorical value that was constitutive of meaning. Metaphor was not imposed upon the world, it unveiled the truth of the world. This is why our understanding of what kind of universe we live in matters so much. If we live in a mostly dead, accidental, purposeless universe, the history of the evolution of consciousness preserved in language is nothing more than a quirky detail about how we came to be what we are. The story might have been otherwise. It says nothing about the world as it is, beyond the anthropological curiosity of the time creatures appeared in the universe who experienced the cosmos poetically—one more odd, random fact in the universe. But if we live in a created universe where mind is ontologically primary, the order of the universe is suffused with purpose. There is more to the story than accidental, purposeless matter (whatever matter is). The connections and relationships between things in the world, and between these things and our feelings and ideas about them, are not merely the inventions of

---

[137] Barfield, *Speaker's Meaning*, 188.
[138] Barfield, *Poetic Diction*, 56.

poets but reveal something about the world our relation to the world. Before the development of the mind's conscious power of abstraction, this unity in relation was directly perceived even if minds were not conscious of the relation as a relation. But a mind can lose its ability to see the unity that is the foundation of real relation. We cannot unlearn our capacity for abstract thought, but we can and should ask how we can nurture our ability to see unity. When poets create true metaphors, their language restores our concept of unity, even if we can no longer directly perceive it. The imagination can re-mind us, literally, of the relationships that inhere in the cosmos. Through the imagination we can learn to see again, achieving that which Eliot called transcendent experience.

There are two forces operating in this developed consciousness. One force splits meaning into separate, isolated concepts. The other perceives resemblances among things and strives to understand what they are. Poets try to express these relations in true metaphors that hint at the living reality torn apart by pure intellect functioning independently of imagination.[139] This is precisely what is meant by the poetic apriori. Metaphors are created by poets. When the metaphors are true, they register something eternal that can be perceived in thought through the operation of both forces of consciousness in one mind—the rational principle, which is conscious of poetry, and the poetic principle, which makes poetry.[140] Consciousness learns to oscillate between these two forces without reducing one to the other. As the oscillation between imaginative reach and contemplative reflection intensifies, poetry is increasingly created from the fullness of self-consciousness.[141]

In a created world, where the universe as a whole has meaning, poets do not create poetry from nothing. They find metaphors that awaken our consciousness of meaning. But they risk error and imprecision when the meanings they try to express reach beyond the definitions of words that reify our fixed ideas about the world. Logic governs the arrangement of stable terms within propositions to eliminate error. But the poetic reaches for fresh meaning from inside individual words, enlivening them through new combinations that allow surprising light to shine on and through the words. In the great poet, just as in the great scientist, rationality must be developed along with imagination's power to reach toward the unfamiliar and the unknown. All great discovery in poetry and science depends upon

---

[139] Barfield, *Poetic Diction*, 88.
[140] Barfield, *Poetic Diction*, 103.
[141] Barfield, *Poetic Diction*, 110.

this. If only one of these forces is developed, the result is bad poetry and bad science: "If the poetic is unduly ascendant, behold the mystic or the madman, unable to grasp the reality of percepts at all—of being still resting, as it were, in the bosom of gods or demons—not yet a man, man in the fullness of his stature, at all. But if the passive, logistic, prosaic principle dominates, then the man becomes—what? the *collector*, the man who cannot grasp the reality of anything *but* percepts."[142]

Philosophical imagination remains open to strangeness in the created universe. It fosters rationality to understand what is discovered along the way. But it also nurtures the force of creative intuition, imagination's power to make revealing metaphors and to perceive analogies, because this is the only way in which consciousness is expanded and knowledge is grown. This is a beautiful and strange world. Our sense of its strangeness arises when we come in contact with consciousnesses besides our own, human or otherwise, initially inspiring wonder and then, as we come to understand something about the strangeness we meet, aesthetic imagination.[143] In a created universe, the conceptual frame for such contact is the analogia entis—an idea that takes the mind to the limits of language. It expresses the meaning of creation, the transcendence of the creator, and the reality of God's analogical immanence in creation. It is the reason for our hope that philosophical imagination can grow in knowledge of the created universe, which also deepens our comprehension of God's incomprehensibility. Because the analogia entis is a kind of knowledge, imperfectly expressed in images, likenesses, and metaphors, it motivates our desire to say the as-yet unsayable, and it turns us toward worship when we break past the limits of language into the fullness of silence where we meet the God beyond analogy.

---

[142] Barfield, *Poetic Diction*, 139.
[143] Barfield, *Poetic Diction*, 177.

X. Imagination and the Analogia Entis

The idea of analogy grew up among the Greeks as they wrestled with the problem of the One and the Many. Parmenides believed everything is one, and all change is illusion. His was a philosophy of absolute identity. Heraclitus denied permanence of being and believed only in becoming. His was a philosophy of absolute flux and difference. Plato and Aristotle brought together these two extremes, each in his own way, by using analogy to understand the meaning of unity given such an obvious diversity of beings in the universe. The idea of the analogia entis matured in Thomas Aquinas's philosophical investigations: if creation is an effect of God, then a metaphysics of creation can neither assert that creation is wholly alien to God nor can it say creation is wholly like the creator. The analogy of being acknowledges both the similarity and the dissimilarity between God and creation. Analogy always falls short, which is why the arc of philosophical imagination ultimately bends toward worshipful silence, but because we are creatures who desire to know, we are compelled to explore both creation and the incomprehensible mystery of God.

Philosophical imagination makes metaphysics possible. In metaphysics, we reach toward reality—toward being in any sense and toward whatever grounds being, if that turns out to be a coherent idea. Questions of being are fundamental, even if our language devolves into silence when we try to articulate the nature of being and whatever lies beyond being. We come to know reality as a whole through acts of philosophical imagination. Our putative acts of knowing might distort reality, or they might reveal partial truth about it. But we have no other vantage point from which to assess the nature of the gap between what is and what we think we know, between reality and our own theories and images of reality, between the apriori and poesis. Reasons inhere in minds, and the truth of reality as a whole can only take hold in a mind. This is why the kind of universe we live in matters. If the universe is an accidental eruption from nothing, with no intended purpose or meaning as a whole, we have no reason to believe that our acts of philosophical imagination bring us closer to knowledge of reality. But if reality itself comes from something like a mind that can be in communion with our own minds, we might have a reason to hope for some degree of concordance between our minds and reality, just as the truth of a poem created by one mind can take hold in another mind, as a kind of communion between those minds. If the universe is created, we might be able to discover the character of the mind that is the source of reality, as our active philosophical imaginations reach toward the fullness of as-yet dark reality. This transforms the act of philosophical imagination into an act of contemplative prayer. The framing idea at the center of this way of conceiving the poetic apriori is the analogia entis.

Because our exploration of the universe always proceeds from within the active philosophical imagination, our philosophical investigations must include not only what is known but also the act of knowing. The act of philosophical imagination is expressed in the content of what we make, but because the act itself is our portal to reality, our insights cannot be separated from the nature of the act itself. The artifacts of this act must, in a sense, be performed for the artifacts to be illuminating: the contours of reality in a created universe require the participation of a mind to light up from within. The act of philosophical imagination is immersed in the fullness of lived experience, where the meaning of the smallest experience gains clarity. The act that allows us to see creation as a gift is not disembodied abstraction but the presence of the entire mind, embodied in the created universe. George MacDonald wrote, "The imagination is that faculty which gives form to thought. The imagination of man is made in the image of the imagination of God. A man has but to light the lamp within the form: his imagination is the light, it is not the form."[144] Erich Przywara calls this a creaturely metaphysics. It dwells between consciousness and being. It is perceived in the movement of becoming as the identity of the not-yet is derived from that toward which it is tending.[145] This is the heart of our hope in the created universe

In the history of philosophical thought, truth, goodness, and beauty have come to be known as transcendentals. Kant thought of transcendentals in relation to things as they are known—the true addressed in *The Critique of Pure Reason*, the good in *The Critique of Practical Reason*, and the beautiful in *The Critique of Judgment*. But the more ancient idea of transcendentals portrays them as relating to things as they are. The divide between antiquity's concept of transcendentals and that of Kant centers on the question of whether our knowledge refers to reality or only to our minds without reference to reality beyond our minds. Thomas Aquinas framed the idea of transcendentals in light of his belief that the world was

---

[144] George MacDonald, *A Dish of Orts*, Forgotten Books, London (2012), 2.

[145] Erich Przywara, *Analogia Entis: Metaphysics, Original Structure, and Univeral Rhythm*, Eerdman's (2014), 124. Throughout this chapter I have included references for authorities to whom Przywara turns for support, in case the original presentations of ideas illuminates Przywara's use of the ideas in building his own argument.

created. Thomas was interested in the relation of the soul to the things in the created world. He believed that truth is the domain of the soul. Truth and falsehood reside in the mind.[146] Goodness and evil inhere in things.[147] Thomas clarified a dialectic between truth and goodness, in which the two are brought together through the commerce between consciousness and being.

Beauty is related to truth and goodness, but it inheres both in the mind that contemplates the beautiful and in beautiful things themselves. This leads to an aesthetics of mind and an aesthetics of matter, both of which are necessary to move from consciousness to ontology (the relationship of transcendentals to things). We want to understand the correlation between consciousness and being in a true creaturely metaphysics that refers to the whole, while illuminating the horizon that lies beyond our own vantage point. The creator beyond our horizon is also the sustainer of that horizon, of our own platform of being, and of our consciousness of being. We see the shapes that appear in our world, constituting the *aposteriori* accessible to observational methods in both daily life and rigorous science. But we also see a unified world, rather than mere shapes. This accessible aposteriori reveals an inner apriori that is the formula of the world, the inner condition for the form of the world. Because the shapes we encounter are shapes of real things, this inner apriori is an inner apriori of the aposteriori. Przywara called it an *aposteriori apriori*.[148]

In our reach for the deepest harmony of this world, we always work from a metaphysics that allows the universe to be a universe, a cosmos with form and order. As humanity unfolds, this metaphysics expands, oscillating between the morphology we study in science and the ideas of things that are revealed through the shapes explored by science. Science is a placeholder for our best way of reaching toward the shapes in the universe, but these demand that we expand our metaphysics—our questions about what the universe is and our questions about why it is what it is. This is a unified act of the imagination that is necessary if we hope to tell a story about the whole. This is the method of the analogia entis, in which we are always attempting to comprehend the whole from within the whole that comprehends us. The analogia entis is formalized in a method through which we comprehend something, and by comprehending it, we become aware of the transcendent above-and-beyond its unity, above-and-beyond

---

[146] Aquinas, *Summa Theologica* I q 82 a 3.
[147] Aquinas, *Questiones Disputatae de Veritate* q1 a2.
[148] Przywara, *Analogia Entis,* 136.

all unity to which we have access. In the same way, the truth that is beyond history reveals itself as being beyond history but does so through history.[149] This is another way of stating the meaning of the poetic apriori—that which is beyond history, revealed through the history we make.

From within an apriori metaphysics, the telos of the universe illuminates the purpose of everything directed toward the end. From within an aposteriori metaphysics, we deduce the ground from things in the world. But both of these arise from within a creaturely metaphysics, and they point to a God beyond creation. The meter of God's poesis rhythmically beats in the poetry of created things. The relation of a created thing to the creator is its inward truth.[150] A creature has a kind of potency toward its end, toward God. As this potency is enacted, a pattern of the divine vision of the whole is revealed. This is the light of the inscape of things expressed by Hopkins in his poetry. It is the eternal form of beauty glimpsed by Plato as he gazed on local beauties in the marketplace. We can only see these patterns if we overcome polarity within our creaturely metaphysics and learn to see essence in-and-beyond existence, God beyond-and-in the creature.

Parmenides's metaphysics was an extreme version of absolute unity. The metaphysics of Heraclitus was an extreme version of absolute movement. In the case of Parmenides' idea of the One, the experience of stability in created things is infinitely extrapolated into an eternal apriori, while Heraclitus's flux is an infinite extrapolation of the experience of change among created things, leaving nothing but the pure aposteriori. The in-and-beyond binds unity and movement together, a *unity* of movement, and a unity of *movement*.[151] The reality of our creaturely being is a dynamism of essence and existence. But a creaturely metaphysics that reaches imaginatively toward the unknown does so because of the hope that the unknown is knowable in the formula of God-beyond-the-creature. Philosophical imagination is always on its way, moving toward the fullness of wisdom rather than possessing it. It is always a knowing in unknowing, an act that moves under the poignant guidance of Augustine's maxim, "If you understand it, it is not God."[152] Philosophical imagination participates in truth, without claiming to arrive at truth's fullness, because our concepts are always overcome by mystery. We enter into the mystery of God so that we

---

[149] Przywara, *Analogia Entis*, 152.
[150] Przywara, *Analogia Entis*, 158.
[151] Przywara, *Analogia Entis*, 159.
[152] Augustine, *Sermons* CVII iii 5.

might more deeply grasp God's incomprehensibility.[153] Thomas believed we reach the summit of our earthly knowledge in the night of God as the unknown.[154] We come to understand the depth of God's invisibility in the depth of God's visibility.[155]

When we try to use language to express what is beyond language, even the best formulations of our ideas disrupt their own unity and completeness. They always fall short. But the search for better ways to express the ineffable is an important and enlivening act of philosophical imagination in a created universe. We continue in hope because of what our minds are at the deepest level—the image and likeness of the divine mind, overcoming the absoluteness of creaturely embeddedness in the pure flux of a world without unity but also overcoming the absolute distance of an apriori One that is beyond participation. At the center of an apriori–aposteriori and aposteriori–apriori metaphysics, the philosophical imagination's fundamental principle is that of the in-and-beyond. This metaphysical principle is called analogy. This form of analogy only makes sense in a created universe: in such a universe, the connection between analogy (*ana-logia*) and being reveals an order that is intended through the act of creation. The resonance of *Logos* in the word analogy points toward the idea of being-as-meaningful in a way that is perceptible by the mind. In this profound form of Augustinian dialectic, the mind moves between critical distance from, and mystical fusion with, truth. Dialectic leads us to fundamental laws only by passing through the passion of this movement, alternating between identity and contradiction. Analogy does not leap into fantasies about dwelling among the gods, nor does it retreat into the miasmal fog of pure immanence. It finds a balance in the confusion that constitutes a kind of spiritual growth in which "defiant self-recusing yields to humble self-discrimination, and passionate desire for fusion to loving self-surrender."[156]

The foundation of the order operative within analogy—a self-ordering within being-ordered— is the principle of non-contradiction.[157] Aristotle first formulated the principle when he argued that something cannot simultaneously both be and not be in the same respect: we cannot, in the same respect, both affirm and deny something. This fundamental principle

---

[153] Augustine, *On the Trinity* XV ii 2.
[154] Aquinas, *Commentary on De Trinitate of Boethius* q1 a2, corp et ad1.
[155] Przywara, *Analogia Entis*, 182.
[156] Przywara, *Analogia Entis*, 196.
[157] Przywara, *Analogia Entis*, 197.

extends both to things as they are (or else as they eventually are, if there is a season of indeterminacy) and to our knowledge of things that exist. Even if everything is denied, this principle cannot be among the denied things, because the principle itself is the foundation for all thinking, including that mode of thought called doubt. Doubt was the starting point for Descartes's method. But long before Descartes, Augustine argued that even the doubt that doubts everything cannot doubt its own doubting. When we doubt, we remember why we doubt, and we understanding that we are doubting. This means that in addition to doubt, we have life, memory, understanding, will, thought, knowledge, and judgment: "For if these things were not, one should be unable to doubt anything at all."[158]

The principle of non-contradiction is preserved by analogy as the most fundamental activity of thought. In pure logic, which focuses on the form of judgment, rather than upon the theme of truth, the principle of non-contradiction is nothing more than an expression of the principle of identity. Hegel's denial of this in his version of dialectic destabilizes the principle of non-contradiction. But even in Hegel, the principle of identity is still operative because apparent contradiction is worked out through higher identities within the immanent world. The principle is operative until Heidegger finally radicalizes Hegelian contradiction into the nothing that determines and produces all things.

The idea of analogy realizes the principle of non-contradiction without reducing it either to pure logic or to dialectic. The principle is the foundation of the struggle between the Heraclitian idea of a never-ending flux of oppositions and the Parmenidean idea of the One without change, the antithetical ideas that all is movement and all is rest. Dialectic must oscillate between the two ideas, but analogy is the middle, the equilibrium that is the principle of non-contradiction grounding all thought: reality comprises both actuality and possibility, and the relationship between the two appears in thought as the concept of analogy, in which an immanent dynamism is directed toward an end. The idea of *telos* prevents analogy from merely signifying a rhythmic oscillation. It carries the idea of analogy beyond immanence and reveals the transcendent meaning of the immanent, the peculiar orientation of creatures in a created universe where the apriori is revealed through the aposteriori, the eternal through that which has been

---

[158] Augustine, *On the Trinity* X x 14.

made. This is the archetype that grounds the idea of the poetic apriori, expressed most completely in the idea of analogy as the immanence of transcendence—the *poiein* understood as *eidos*.[159]

The transcendent is ontologically prior to the immanent. When truth, goodness, and beauty appear in the immanent sphere, they are grounded not in the immanent but in the eternal. The relationship of participation between creature and creator, which is a gift imparted from above, is the crux of analogy. It illuminates the cause and the meaning of the being of all things, in which immanence is intimately related to transcendence. Being is inward to all things, and all being is from God: "Hence it must be that God is in all things, inwardly."[160] At this highest point, analogy expresses the dynamic movement between a transcending immanence and an indwelling transcendence.[161]

Plato conceived of an uncreated world of essences. But analogy points to the creative essence of God as the origin of potentiality in the world, giving limits—which is to say, form—to creatures. This is why creatures, though utterly dependent upon their relation to the creator, are not oriented toward nothingness. The directedness of creation, its telos, follows from this relation between the imminent and the transcendent. In Thomas's formulation of analogy, creatures are willed for their own sakes as much as for the sake of God. They reveal God, expressing something positive, mysterious, and eternal, rather than descending back into the nothingness from which they came.[162] The analogical relationship between creature and creator is why the supernatural perfects the natural, fulfilling our spiritual desire as creation proceeds toward its fitting end. The beatific vision is inextricably related to the fullness of creaturely flourishing.

The initiating mystery of God is this: we are created and sustained by God, and yet we are so far from identity with God that we can still say No to the divine will. Analogy requires and reveals this mystery. It allows us to attribute things to God, while also acknowledging God's absolute otherness. When we perceive negation, we always do so in relationship to something we have affirmed, which is why the theological *via negative*

---

[159] Przywara, *Analogia Entis*, 210.
[160] Aquinas, *Summa Theologica* I q8 a1 corp.
[161] Przywara, *Analogia Entis*, 216.
[162] Przywara, *Analogia Entis*, 224. Thomas wrote: "It is the same to say that God made creatures for himself and that he will have made them for the sake of their own being" (*Disputed Questions on the Power of God* q5 a4 corp).

cannot be the whole story. We can deny something about God only if we have some positive knowledge of God.[163] But this analogy of alterity, in which every similarity leads to awareness of an even greater dissimilarity, is the deepest knowledge of God we can have in this life. Analogy's affirmation of the relationship between creator and creature is not a claim that we can come to full knowledge of God. Thomas has a clear formulation of this point: "We are said, at the pinnacle of our knowledge, to know God as unknown, because the mind is found to have entered most perfectly into the knowledge of God when it knows his essence to be beyond everything that it is able to comprehend in the conditions of this life."[164]

Being—the entis of analogia entis—is the ultimate structure encompassing everything that is. In one direction, it spans the distance between everything that is and pure nothingness. In the other direction it spans the distance from everything that is to the threshold of the divine Is, in comparison to which creaturely being looks like nothing.[165] Because creatures are created out of nothing, they find their authentic relation to the creator by appearing as nothing against the divine Is. Analogy resides between being and nothingness, between God and creature. The community of creator and creature is preserved by analogy, because within it the nothingness of the creature is called being analogously.[166]

In the *Symposium*, Plato described the power of eros to break through to the transcendent. Eros is the hunter that traverses all things and makes the world fruitful.[167] The force of eros hunts its way through the particulars of the world, moving from individual beauties to beauty in itself, the form of beauty that instigates the hunter's longing for home in the first place. But there is a paradox in the Platonic view of the divine. He made this explicit in the *Euthyphro* where the divine appears to be both primordially creative in relation to the archetypal forms and dependent upon the archetypal forms as antecedent to divine creativity. Plato asks, "Is that which is holy, holy because the gods love it, or do the gods love it because it is holy?"[168] Vacillation between the poles of this mystery is the heart of Plato's version of analogy. As Thomas developed his own ideas about the relation between creator and creature, he borrowed Plato's images of the

---

[163] Aquinas, *Disputed Questions on the Power of God* q7 a5 corp.
[164] Aquinas, *Commentary on De Trinitate of Boethius* q1 a2 ad1.
[165] Przywara, *Analogia Entis*, 236.
[166] Aquinas, *Questiones Disputatae de Veritate* q2 a11 ad5.
[167] Plato, *Symposium* 203b–d.
[168] Plato, *Euthyphro* 10a.

artist (*artifex*), the artist's idea (*idea atificis*), and the work of art (*artificiatum*). The images can only function as analogies for the mystery of what occurs between the creator and the creature, but they are nonetheless the only way we can understand the relationship between creator and creature.

We are creatures, and we can only see from the perspective of creation. But from that perspective, we can turn inward, focusing not on our minds and souls as such but instead looking through the functions of our minds and souls in their acts of artistic creation, virtue, contemplation, and so forth. In this act of the philosophical imagination, we look away from self and toward the eternal truth of God. We orient ourselves toward the ever above-and-beyond. This is the rhythm of the rational soul. We come to know God precisely through our faltering attempts to ascend toward comprehension. At the same time, this Augustinian view of the mystery of mind imagines the mind as a mirror that allows us to see but in such a way that we come to know the mirror, rather than God-as-God-is: "You may be able to learn what is proper to yourself: but can you ever learn what—whatever it may be—is proper to him who made you?"[169]

Even in relation to the things of creation, the rhythm is a rhythm of coming to be, or else a rhythm of having been: "Before they might be they are not, and when they are they are fleeing away, and when they are fled they no longer are."[170] The harmony of the whole emerges as contrasting things come together in the unity we call beauty, which is created from the opposition of contraries in the world.[171] This movement of coming to be and passing away within a created world manifests the mystery of the God who creates and sustains it. Creatures are fundamentally mutable, oscillating between antitheses. But in this oscillation, creation opens to the mystery of God who contains all things. Analogy best reveals God when the most creaturely aspect of the creature, its nothingness, is viewed in the light of its origin and source of sustenance, the God who Is.[172]

Our knowledge of ourselves, of each other, and of all that comprises our experience of life is a lighted ambiguity, a form of illumination that reveals absurdity as much as it reveals ecstasy. We are suspended in God and utterly dependent. The mystery is that this suspension is only possible because the creaturely abyss of emptiness and the groundlessness of God

---

[169] Augustine, *Sermons* 52, 10, 23.
[170] Augustine, *De Libero Arbitrio* III vii 21.
[171] Augustine, *City of God* XI xviii.
[172] Przywara, *Analogia Entis*, 266.

are incomprehensibly one. Creatures reveal the mystery of God, the superluminous darkness of God, because they stand only by standing beyond themselves. Augustinian analogy focuses on the creature as suspended in relation to the creator. Thomist analogy moves from this suspendedness to the order of the universe as a holy order. Apart from this holy order, isolated things related to each other only in an accidental way can disintegrate into mere antithesis. But within the holy order, the potential for disintegration is overcome by the unity of the whole that comes from God.

The suspended realities of world and spirit reveal the holiness of order in the cosmos, the unity of the universe as a transcendent relation rather than merely the sum of isolated and countable things in the immanent world. From inside the universe, each particular thing has its own explanation. But the reality of the whole—and even the mere existence of the whole as a whole—cannot be explained from within. Suspendedness points beyond the immanent universe to a creator who is not merely one more link in a chain of explanations connecting all the relations within the universe but who is, rather, the ground of this unified order, the condition for the very existence of such order. In one sense, because God is transcendent, God is outside every order in the universe. But in another sense, God permeates it as its creator and sustainer, making the order itself sacred.

In a created universe, the idea of a holy order that orients the universe as a whole transforms the frame in which we understand sense experience. For Thomas, the natural knowledge available to creatures like us is limited by what we can access through sense experience.[173] Whether we are doing science, philosophy, or theology, imagination and language can only function in human terms, which means according to what we receive through our senses. God is beyond anything our intellects can represent on their own.[174] This limit is so complete that even our mystical experiences of God are subject to it. Whatever light or dazzling darkness we mystically encounter is constrained by our nature, and the sense-conditioned knowledge of the mystic must, in the end, be an experience of the unknown God.[175]

Our dependence on our senses for knowledge limits our minds, but it also profoundly transforms the significance of sense experience and the meaning of nature itself, from which our experience is derived. When we

---

[173] Aquinas, *Summa Theologica* I q12 a12.
[174] Aquinas, *Questiones Disputatae de Veritate* q8 a1 ad8.
[175] Przywara, *Analogia Entis,* 383.

see that isolated things within the universe are related to a holy and transcendent order, we can understand the freedom of our own actions. Order is imposed in accord with the potential that is given to us in a material world. This potential is not determined by some accidental relation among immanent things. Rather, it derives from a freedom made possible by the nothingness of creation, in the sense of its complete dependence upon the creator: "Insofar as something comes from nothing, it follows that it is ... labile."[176] The analogia entis reveals the basis of this freedom, because a creature becomes what it is in the space between its own dependent nothingness and the transcendence of God beyond all things—the origin of all principal and of the totality of being. God is not a being among beings. Analogy expresses the lability of a creature on its way to becoming in a created universe where hope is grounded in a creator who is beyond all thing-ness, who is no-thing not because of a paucity of being but because of a superabundance.

This freedom enables the creature to be on the way toward what it most fully is. It represents a kind of possibility that can be influenced without being over-determined. Thomas thought of it as movement toward the beautiful, that which is complete in itself. He portrayed God as an artist and conceived of the beautiful as the most emphatic expression of the true and the good, in equal measure. In its absolute sense, perfect beauty is convertible with God who is the foundation of beauty's dynamism.[177] Its dynamism moves from nothing to nothing, as music moves from silence to silence. This is simply to say that beauty manifests in form, and form is defined by limit. Because a limit is the end of a thing and the beginning of nothing, beauty is also an expression of creaturely frailty.

A universe oriented toward God tends toward the balance characteristic of order. But this greater order, originating from that which is above-and-beyond, can disrupt smaller forms of order that exist within a closed system. We each exist as closed systems because of the limits constitutive of form and because our intellects are bound to sense experience. But from this vantage point we become conscious of something beyond ourselves: we see our relation to the transcendent, as creature related to creator. We begin by reaching toward ideas that are approximations of God, the origin of both the unity of the cosmos and the multiplicity of appearance in the

---

[176] Aquinas, *De Malo* q16 a6 ad5.
[177] Przywara, *Analogia Entis*, 286–287.

world.[178] But we only recognize God as God when we go beyond Anselm's formulation of God as *that than which nothing greater can be thought* and recognize God as that being who is beyond anything that can be thought: "This is the ultimate human knowledge of God: to know that one does not know God."[179]

But this is not the end of the story. Through intellect and imagination, we can reach beyond the immediate experience of sense toward a higher vision of God that is our greatest good, though our nature is not sufficient to attain it on its own.[180] To reach this vision, our nature must be elevated to place in which such an end is fitting for us.[181] In this life we are naturally inclined toward this supernatural vision, and our desires remain restless and unsatisfied until we reach this highest point.[182] This hope depends upon the created nature of the cosmos, which transforms our understanding of everything that shows up in the universe, including our minds, inclinations, and imaginations. Our restlessness is intensified by our awareness of the above-and-beyond that manifests within the things of creation. Though our vision of God reveals the incomprehensibility of God, nonetheless because creation is God's self-communication, once we learn to see the universe as being from God, all experience is transformed, and we grow into a new way of contemplating even the smallest part of the cosmos.[183]

This brings us back to the philosophical question of self-knowledge in light of analogy's defining idea—the idea of the middle. Analogy illuminates reality for us because our own inwardness is an immanent middle linking creation to the transcendent. Our conscious life is situated between the placeholder frames of the material and spiritual, in a kind of suspendedness that is itself an image of a greater reality. The human soul becomes all things as it receives the cosmos through sense and intellect, and by having this knowledge, we "approach the likeness of God, in whom all things exist."[184] But this image of our souls as an immanent middle points beyond itself, because the true middle is God, the highest summit in whom all multiplicity and antitheses are one.

---

[178] Aquinas, *Summa Theologica* I q13 a4 ad3.
[179] Aquinas, *Disputed Questions on the Power of God* q7 a5 ad14.
[180] Aquinas, *De Malo* q5 a1.
[181] Aquinas, *Questiones Disputatae de Veritate* q27 a2.
[182] Aquinas, *Summa Contra Gentiles* III 50.
[183] Przywara, *Analogia Entis,* 291.
[184] Aquinas, *Summa Theologica* I q80 a1.

We come to understand this in the only way that we can—by ever more fully understanding ourselves as a creaturely form of a mediating middle. We are rational souls united to bodies, a perfection insofar as a human is made up of all things: "Man is said to be a little world, since all the creatures in the world are in a certain way found in him."[185] Thomas thought of us as little worlds because of our knowledge of reality, but we are learning about fascinating physical ways in which something similar can be said. Our carbon-based life is built upon a substance that is made only in stars, and we exist physically composed of stardust. The adventure of our life evolves out of this richness. It is an adventure that is always on the way but one filled with hope because of its telos. Thomas's analogical thought culminates in the analogia entis, precisely because the entis signifies the unfathomable separation between God and creature but also provides the nexus from which radical unity is declared. His development of the idea of the analogia entis reveals humanity as a border where nature and spirit meet, and it illuminates the created world as a cosmos.[186]

As an expression of the principle of non-contradiction, the analogia entis is a radical starting point. Within the analogia entis, thought is its own starting point. In the history of philosophy, thinkers have sought evermore original starting points, but each one has interpreted the principle of non-contradiction, rather than taking the principal as its foundation. The natural philosophers began with the primordial elements, Anaxagoras with the mind, Plato with mind's object (eidos), Aristotle with the subjective act of the mind (*noesis*), Descartes with the isolated act of the mind enclosed in the *cogito*, Kant with the transcendental form of the mind's act as such, Hegel with the three-part dynamism of this form, and Husserl with the ultimate irreducibility of the objective and intentional forms of the mind's acts. But in each of these cases, the so-called starting point ended up in a self-referential circle: either it must be assumed to establish itself or else it is merely asserted as true, a kind of *clinamen* about which the philosopher begs, "Give me only this and all else follows." The analogia entis, as nothing more than the form of the principle of non-contradiction, is a condition for thought established in the mere act of thought. It is a thoroughly creaturely principle that expresses only the complete potentiality of the creature, an openness that allows the creature to experience the cosmos as pointing through itself, and beyond itself, to God.[187]

---

[185] Aquinas, *Summa Theologica* I q91 a1.
[186] Przywara, *Analogia Entis*, 305.
[187] Przywara, *Analogia Entis*, 310.

There is a kind of *cogito ergo sum* in the analogia entis, in which thought returns into itself. But in the Cartesian formulation, the mind turns back merely to its own act as a mind without reference to the object with which the mind is engaged, or else it merely notes the object as it relates to the self-reflecting, active mind. The formulation of this return of thought to itself in the analogia entis illuminates intension toward all objects as the essential nature of the active mind. In knowing its own act, the mind knows the nature of its act, and by knowing the nature of its act, it knows its own essential nature—the fundamental capacity to conform to things.[188] In this radically non-Cartesian formulation of the cogito, intention within an act of the mind is not directed toward a mere object that is imminent to this act but rather toward a fully existing thing: the act of intension lights up the truth of things. This illuminated truth is not located within the isolated cogito. Its location is always the occasion of the existing thing, though which the transcendent in the immanent is disclosed. When creaturely consciousness correlates with the being of an existing thing in this way, the intending mind is able see the light of the in-and-beyond.[189] This act is the mind's experience of the analogia entis. The imaginative expression of what is seen in this irreducible act constitutes the poetic apriori.

As a principle within the cogito, the analogia entis compels us to examine the objective facts of the created world and to see through-and-beyond everything with the faith available to minds in a created world, where the unity of the uni-verse is a coherent concept. This unity, fulfilled in the creator, motivates the idea that our insight into reality is grounded in the principle of non-contradiction, in which it is impossible to make contradictory true assertions regarding the same thing. Pythagoras discovered a cosmos that vibrates with a resonant rhythm. In this mysterious sense of the music of the universe, the rhythm of being is the rhythm of analogy, and the rhythm of analogy is the rhythm of thought. But just as musical rhythms require the notes, along with the silences that come before, between, and beyond the notes, the analogia entis as being and as thought passes into the silence that is the incomprehensibility of God: "The 'resonant analogy' is fulfilled in this 'silent analogy'."[190]

As embodied minds move through the universe of concretely individual things, creation's unity expresses itself to our minds. Unity underlies the individual things, but it also reveals itself through these things and

---

[188] Aquinas, *Questiones Disputatae de Veritate* q1 a9.
[189] Przywara, *Analogia Entis*, 312.
[190] Przywara, *Analogia Entis*, 314.

within these things as an immanent transcendent. This is metaphysical experience. This is where thought begins. The rhythm of thought leads our minds from the experience of the immanent transcendent to awareness of ourselves as beings capable of thought. From there we become aware of the transcending immanence of our own consciousness of being. Our most profound questions about what underlies all being arise from this rhythm of metaphysical experience, because the rhythm always moves from the immanent to what lies beyond, oscillating between the transcending immanence described by Augustine and the indwelling transcendence described by Thomas. The structure of this oscillating rhythm is analogy, which appears in both metaphysics and religion—the consciousness of the interval between creator and creature, disclosing ever-greater dissimilarity within every similarity, whether that similarity manifests as a likeness, an image, or a word.[191]

Augustine described the mystery of our inwardness that leads our intuitions beyond that inwardness toward the unfathomable mystery of God. Thomas described an indwelling transcendence, wherein the creator and creation are fused in such a way that we are rooted in God and in the tangible universe: we are creatures hanging in infinite space, for whom the heights and depths of God are beyond comprehension. In both cases religion is analogy, because God always ruptures the wineskins of our inwardness, sending us to the ever-greater but without destroying us. Our suspendedness in God uproots any fixity of our place in the palpable universe. There is no system that is not finally exceeded by the path along which analogy carries us. Augustine said that if we ever believe we have comprehended God, we can be sure it is not God whom we have comprehended. Analogical philosophy never arrives at completeness, because it always points toward a God who can only be encountered through analogy, which is always on the way.[192]

Thomas's philosophy resides between that of the pure image and that of the pure concept. In his philosophy, what is sensible in images, symbols, myths, and mysteries is both a necessary portal into the intelligible world and the only realm within which our knowledge of the intelligible world is possible. The sensible phenomenal world points toward the world of the Logos. This becomes transparent as our knowledge grows, moving ana-

---

[191] Przywara, *Analogia Entis*, 424.
[192] Przywara, *Analogia Entis*, 429.

logically from a similarity, however great, toward the ever greater dissimilarity of the divine ground of this phenomenal world. Analogical philosophy overcomes the opposition between the philosophies of pure concept and pure image, ascending from images to the Logos using symbols, myths, and mysteries, and descending from the Logos to the image by way of the same. It avoids both the bathos of isolated images and the conceptually abstract purity of an isolated Logos.[193]

In the progress from image to Logos and the regress from Logos to image, the turning point is constituted by myth and mystery, out of which we philosophize. Platonic philosophy shows this Logos developing consciously out of mythos and mysterium. Aristotle was critical of the Platonic myths, and instead embraced the approach of rational demonstration. But he retained the Platonic myth of Eros, and he portrayed the movement of the cosmos as a movement between lovers. Logos is being in-and-beyond image, myth, and mystery. Because of the in-and-beyond of creaturely essence and existence, all creaturely being is analogy of being. Likewise, because we can only conceive of Logos as the in-and-beyond of mythos and mysterium, we have no creaturely Logos other than analogy as Logos: philosophy in the Logos is a creaturely philosophy.[194] For creatures like us, being and Logos can only be understood through analogy.

The movement from image to Logos and back is the analogical movement at the heart of the deepest work the philosophical imagination was created to do. It begins where it must begin, among the things in an inherently meaningful world, which is to say a created world. And beginning with the experience of created things as inherently meaningful, it must reach toward what lies beyond and ever beyond. We work out the fundamental structures of reality through what we make in our philosophical imaginations, and we revise as we grow in our consciousness of the apriori that lies beyond our current knowledge and experience. We reach with our imaginations. We reach again and again, always falling short but remaining hopeful. This is the adventure of the philosophical imagination that is always on the way in a meaningful universe. The philosophical imagination's experience of the cosmos as meaningful and filled with things that point in-and-beyond themselves, explored through the imagination's many forms of creative response to reality, is what I mean by the *poetic apriori*.

---

[193] Przywara, *Analogia Entis*, 434.
[194] Przywara, *Analogia Entis*, 453.

Bibliography

Dante Alighieri, *Il Convivio (The Banquet)*, trans. Richard H. Lansing. Garland Library of Medieval Literature, Ser. B. N (1990).

Dante Alighieri, *The Divine Comedy*, trans. John Ciardi, W.W. Norton, New York (1970).

Thomas Aquinas, *Summa Theologica*, trans. Fathers of the English Dominican Province, Benziger Bros., New York (1981).

Owen Barfield, *Poetic Diction: A Study in Meaning*, Wesleyan University Press, Connecticut (1973).

Owen Barfield, *The Rediscovery of Meaning*, The Barfield Press, California (1977).

Owen Barfield, *Speaker's Meaning*, Barfield Press, Oxford (2011).

Henri Bergson, *Two Sources of Morality and Religion*, trans. Ashley Audra and Cloudesley Brereton, University of Notre Dame, Indiana (1977).

William Blake, *The Complete Poetry and Prose of William Blake*, ed. David V. Erdman, Doubleday, New York (1988).

Benedetto Croce, *The Philosophy of Giamattista Vico*, trans. R.G. Collingwood, H. Lattimer, London (1913).

Thomas Stearns Eliot, *Knowledge and Experience in the Philosophy of F.H. Bradley*, Columbia University Press, New York (1989).

Albert Einstein, *The World as I See It*, John Lane, London (1935).

Thomas Stearns Eliot, *T.S. Eliot: The Complete Poems and Plays*, Harcourt, Brace, Jovanovich, New York (1978).

Austin Farrar, *The Glass of Vision*, Glasgow University Press, Glasgow (1948).

Georg Wilhelm Friedrich Hegel, *The Science of Logic*, trans. George Di Giovanni, Cambridge University Press, Cambridge (2015).

Martin Heidegger, *An Introduction to Metaphysics*, trans. Gregory Fried and Richard Polt, Yale University Press, Connecticut and London (2014).

Gerard Manley Hopkins, *The Major Works*, ed. Catherine Phillips, Oxford University Press, Oxford (2009).

Thomas Kelly, *Testament of Devotion*, HarperOne, New York (1996).

Justus George Lawler, *Hopkins Re-constructed*, Continuum, New York (1998).

Gottfried Wilhelm Leibniz, *The Monadology and Other Philosophical Writings*, trans. Robert Latta, Kessinger Publishing, Montana (2010).

Henri De Lubac, *The Discovery of God*, trans. Alexander Dru, William B. Eerdmans, Michigan (1996).

George MacDonald, *A Dish of Orts*, Forgotten Books, London (2012).

Ric Machuga, *In Defense of the Soul: What it Means to Be Human*, Brazos Press, Michigan (2002).

Charles Peguy, *The Portal of the Mystery of Hope*, trans. David Louis Schindler, Jr. and William B. Eerdmans, Michigan (1996).

Erich Przywara, *Analogia Entis: Metaphysics, Original Structure, and Univeral Rhythm*, Eerdman's (2014).

Erwin Schrodinger, *My View of the World*, Cambridge University Press, Cambridge (1964).

Wallace Stevens, *Collected Poetry and Prose*, ed. Frank Kermode and Joan Richardson, Library of America, New York (1997).

Donald Verene, *Vico's New Science: A Philosophical Commentary*, Cornell University Press, New York (2015).

Donald Verene, *Vico's Science of Imagination*, Cornell University Press, New York (1981).

Giambattista Vico, *The Autobiography of Giambattista Vico*, trans. Max Harold Fisch and Thomas Goddard Bergin, Cornell University Press, New York (1944).

Giambattista Vico, *The New Science*, trans. Thomas Goddard Bergin and Max Harold Fisch, Cornell University Press, New York (1994).

Giambattista Vico, *On the Most Ancient Wisdom of the Italians*, trans. L.M. Palmer, Cornell University Press, New York (1988).

Hans Urs von Balthasar, *The Glory of the Lord: A Theological Aesthetics, III, Studies in Theological Style: Lay Styles*, trans. Oliver Davies, Andrew Louth, Brian McMeil, John Saward, and Rowan Williams, Ignatius Press, California (1986).

Hans Urs von Balthasar, *The Glory of the Lord: A Theological Aesthetics, V, The Realm of Metaphysics in the Modern Age*, trans. Oliver Davies, Andrew Louth, Brian McMeil, John Saward, and Rowan Williams, Ignatius Press, California (1991).

Simone Weil, *Gravity and Grace*, trans. Emma Crawford and Marion von der Ruhr, Routledge Press, New York (1999).

Alfred North Whitehead, *Adventures of Ideas*, Free Press, New York (1967).

Alfred North Whitehead, *Modes of Thought*, Free Press, New York (1966).

Alfred North Whitehead, *Process and Reality*, Free Press, New York (1978).

Charles Williams, *The Figure of Beatrice*, D.S. Brewer, Cambridge (1994).

Ludwig Wittgenstein, *Tractatus Logico-Philosophicus*, trans. Charles Kay Ogden, Routledge Press, New York (1981).

Frances A. Yates, *The Art of Memory*, University of Chicago Press, Illinois (1966).

Adam Zagajewski, "Auto Mirror," in *A Book of Luminous Things*, ed. Czeslaw Milosz, Harcourt, New York (1996).

Index

A

Adam. *See also* Genesis 19, 35, 90, 166
Alighieri, Dante. *See also* art (artificatium) and Dante 56, 57, 59, 60, 165
analogia entis 10–12, 20, 27, 33, 34, 46, 86, 93–95, 102, 107, 109, 110, 114, 115, 147, 149–151, 156, 159, 161, 162
analogical distance 11
analogy 10, 12, 20, 22, 30, 32, 33, 39, 70, 81, 86, 87, 108, 118, 145, 147, 149, 153–156, 158, 160, 162–164
Anselm 34, 36–41, 43, 105, 106, 108, 111, 160
aposteriori apriori 151
Aquinas, Thomas 10, 29–31, 55, 56, 60, 64, 70, 76, 78, 79, 117, 149–151, 153, 155, 156, 158–162, 165
Aristotle 22–25, 55, 59, 60, 67, 117, 149, 153, 161, 164
art (artificiatum) 9, 52, 57, 63, 69, 74–78, 81, 103, 112, 117, 118, 134, 142, 157
  and Bruno 11, 75, 78–82, 103, 106, 115, 127
  and Dante 11, 41, 53, 55–62, 67, 72, 74, 99, 100, 103, 165
  and Lull 75, 76
  of memory 11, 69, 72, 75, 77, 78
  of the poetic apriori 9, 13, 20, 26, 29, 44, 48, 81, 95, 112, 152, 155

religious 22, 52, 53, 106, 124, 139
artist (artifex) 82, 117, 142, 157, 159

B

Barfield, Owen 12, 141–147, 165
body 22, 25, 26, 30, 63, 94, 99, 103, 116, 118, 122
Bruno, Giordano. *See also* Camillo, Giullo; Lull, Raymon 11, 75, 78–82, 103, 106, 115, 127

C

Camillo, Giullo. *See also* Bruno, Giordano; Lull, Raymon 11, 75–78
cogito 161, 162
created world 11, 29, 33, 53, 61, 81, 87, 88, 91, 95, 96, 99, 111, 118, 132, 146, 151, 157, 161, 162, 164
  and Gerard Manley Hopkins 11, 85, 89, 165
  and Wallace Stevens 12, 96, 99, 113, 137, 166

D

Descartes, René. *See also* Cartesian philosophy 67, 122, 127, 154, 161
Donne, John 136

E

eidos 155, 161

Einstein, Albert. *See also* science 122, 124, 165
Eliot, T. S. 12, 133–140, 145, 146, 165
enthymemes 67, 68

F

factum/verum 69, 70, 73
Farrar, Austin 34, 40, 81, 165
fiction 9, 12, 21, 31, 57, 99, 108, 111, 112, 117, 138
    God as 12, 30, 33, 38, 64, 83, 104, 153, 155, 156, 159, 160
    Supreme Fiction 138

G

Genesis. *See also* Adam 19, 137
    Garden of Eden 90

H

haecceitas 91
happiness 30, 44, 58, 81, 96
Heidegger, Martin 15, 154, 165
Heraclitus 114, 125, 149, 152
Hoffman, Donald D. 140, 141
Hopkins, Gerard Manley 11, 12, 85–89, 91–96, 99, 102, 109, 110, 112, 152, 165
humility 32, 43, 44, 55, 81, 93, 115, 119
    and Alfred North Whitehead 12, 93, 113, 118, 123, 166

I

immanence 33, 127, 147, 153, 154, 155, 163

J

Jesus 92

K

Kant, Immanuel 9, 36, 127, 134, 150, 161
Kelly, Thomas 11, 43, 45, 46, 48, 165

L

language 11, 12, 23, 25, 33, 39, 46, 59, 62, 63, 69, 71, 73, 74, 81, 85, 86, 94, 95, 110, 113, 118, 119, 122, 123, 127, 130, 134, 137, 143–145, 147, 149, 153, 158
    naming 19, 21, 29–31, 46, 134, 137, 139
    nature as 29, 47, 63, 106, 142
Leibniz, Gottfried Wilhelm 15, 16, 39, 165
Lewis 46
Logos 13, 153, 163, 164
Lull, Raymon. *See also* Bruno, Giordano; Camillo, Giullo 75, 76

M

MacDonald, George 46–50, 140, 150, 165
memory 11, 20, 69, 74–80, 82, 99, 114, 116, 131, 143, 154
    Theater of Memory 76
metaphor 22, 29, 34, 47, 63, 70, 71, 73, 81, 87, 88, 107, 115, 132, 145
metaphysics, metaphysical 9, 10, 15, 29, 33, 34, 41, 46, 60, 69, 70, 72, 73, 81, 87, 88, 103, 108, 111, 116, 118, 123, 127, 129, 130, 132, 138, 139, 149, 150–153, 163

N

Newman, John Henry 91

P

Parmenides 125, 131, 149, 152
 Paremenidean One 87
Peguy, Charles 11, 50–52, 166
philosophical imagination 9–11, 13, 15, 16, 18, 20–22, 26, 29, 33, 34, 43, 46, 56, 61, 64, 70, 73–75, 80–82, 86, 87, 96, 108, 115, 118–120, 129, 140, 144, 147, 149, 150, 153, 157, 164
 and the poetic imagination 71, 102, 140
 in a created universe 11, 12, 20, 34, 46, 50, 63, 108, 142, 145, 150, 153, 154, 159
paradox. *See also* paradox 45, 70, 108, 156
Plato 39, 59, 100, 104, 124, 126, 127, 131, 142, 149, 152, 155, 156, 161
 Platonic universe 96
 Neoplatonists 142
 Platonic myth 164
poesis 19, 69, 70, 104, 142, 149, 152
poetic apriori 9, 20, 27, 29, 34, 46, 63, 73, 77, 96, 108, 132, 146, 150, 162, 164
poiein 155
prayer 19, 32, 39, 43, 89, 104, 124, 150
 prayer-shaped imagination 89
prudence 73
Przywara, Erich 150–153, 155–164, 166

R

radiance 30, 32, 43, 46, 52, 61–63, 85–87, 89, 102
 of the created world 46, 85, 162
rationality 10, 21, 26, 27, 72, 124, 146, 147
 irrationality 104
realism 70, 141

S

sapienza poetica. *See also* Vico, Giambattista 29
Schrodinger, Erwin 110, 111, 166
science 9, 17, 22–24, 26, 32, 47–49, 72, 73, 106, 110, 111, 115, 116, 122, 125, 130, 140, 141, 146, 151, 158
Scripture 32, 64
Shakespeare, William 70
sin 57, 58
skepticism 23, 106
Socrates 53, 56, 71, 115
Stevens, Wallace 23, 106

T

telos 21, 112, 117, 152, 154, 155, 161
topoi 69, 72–74
transcendence. *See also* immanence 33, 35, 108, 147, 155, 159, 163

U

Urs von Balthasar, Hans 31, 52, 53, 57, 62, 166

V

verum. *See* factum/verum 69, 70, 73
Vico, Giambattista. *See also* sapienza poetica 11, 29, 67, 69, 70–74, 103, 114, 135, 145, 165, 166

W

Whitehead, Alfred North 12, 113–121, 123–130, 132

Z

Zagajewski, Adam 35, 166
Auto Mirror 35, 166

ibidem.eu